The Intuitive Empath

A unique guide on how highly sensitive people can heal psychologically and spiritually. Learn ways to use your gift of intuition and go from surviving to thriving

© **Copyright 2019 - All rights reserved.**

The content contained within this book may not be reproduced, duplicated or transmitted without direct written permission from the author or the publisher.

Under no circumstances will any blame or legal responsibility be held against the publisher, or author, for any damages, reparation, or monetary loss due to the information contained within this book. Either directly or indirectly.

Legal Notice:

This book is copyright protected. This book is only for personal use. You cannot amend, distribute, sell, use, quote or paraphrase any part, or the content within this book, without the consent of the author or publisher.

Disclaimer Notice:

Please note the information contained within this document is for educational and entertainment purposes only. All effort has been executed to present accurate, up to date, and reliable, complete information. No warranties of any kind are declared or implied. Readers acknowledge that the author is not engaging in the rendering of legal, financial, medical or professional advice. The content within this book has been derived from various sources. Please consult a licensed professional before attempting any techniques outlined in this book.

By reading this document, the reader agrees that under no circumstances is the author responsible for any losses, direct or indirect, which are incurred as a result of the use of information contained within this document, including, but not limited to, — errors, omissions, or inaccuracies.

Table of Contents

Table of Contents

Introduction

Chapter 1: Innerstanding Your Empathic Gifts and Challenges

The Empath Personality
The Artist, Creative, and Visionary
The Musician, Performer, and Storyteller
The Dreamer, Seer, and Psychic
The Healer, Counselor, and Therapist
The Carer, Social or Support Worker, and Companion
The Animal Whisperer, Charity Worker, and Volunteer
The Tarot Reader, Spiritual Healer, and Energy Worker
The Independent Worker and 'Self-Employed One'

The Different Types of Empath
Emotional Empaths
Intellectual Empaths
Intuitive Empaths
Psychic or Medical Empaths
Spiritual Empaths
Animal Empaths
Plant Empaths
Environmental Empaths
Introverted Empaths
Activist Empaths

The Science of Empathy
Neurological Activity and Neuroscience
Electromagnetic Energy Fields
Dopamine and Synesthesia

Empath Struggles
Childhood Wounds
The Shadow Self
The Wound of the Soul

Chapter 2: How to Manage Your Energy

Innerstanding What is Yours

The Importance of Boundaries and Grounding

How to Protect your Energy: Techniques and Exercises!
Aura protection exercises
Tree meditation for inner grounding
Crystal Meditation/Connecting to Special Gemstones
Creating a Chi Ball
A short exercise for self-love

Psychic Awareness exercises

Chapter 3: The Physical Body

Lifestyle and Energy
How to heal psychologically
How to heal spiritually
How to heal physically

The Importance of Diet
5 Elements Theory of Chinese Medicine

Food and Emotions
Mindful Empathic Eating

Chapter 4: The Mental Body

Intuition and Psychic Ability

Mental Boundaries
Meditation
Mindfulness

Social Situations and Society

Chapter 5: The Emotional Body

The Importance of Inner Balance

How to Deal with Emotional Overload

Famous (Emotional) Empaths
Mahatma Gandhi
Claiborne Paul Ellis
Hilary Swank

Chapter 6: The Spiritual Body

Cleansing, Clearing, and Alignment
The Astral Body
The Etheric Body
The Soul

The Importance of Discernment
A Stranger's Shoulder to Cry On
An Emotional Dump Ground
A Narcissist, Energy Vampire or Toxic Person Magnet

Chapter 7: Innerstanding the Dynamics between an Empath and Narcissists and Energy Vampires

Narcissists and Energy Vampires: Who are they?

The Empath-Narcissist Relationship

Taking Back Your Power!

Chapter 8: How to Use Your Gifts to Help Others and the World

The Beautiful Gift of Empathy
  Best Careers for an Empath

The Chakra System: Creating Harmony and Wholeness Within
  The Root or Base Chakra
  The Sacral Chakra
  The Solar Plexus Chakra
  Heart Chakra
  Throat Chakra
  Third Eye or Brow Chakra
  Crown Chakra
  How to Heal Your Chakras: A Short Exercise

Kundalini and Wholeness: The Journey of Completion

Conclusion

References

Introduction

Empathy is a beautiful gift. Yet in an often cold and hard world it can sometimes be too much for a sensitive empath with a heightened sense of intuition and emotional connection to cope and survive, and thrive.

As an empath, you have some unique and special strengths. Because of your sensitivity to external influence, and often less than strong boundaries, you become prone to attracting and letting in unwanted energies. Empaths absorb the feelings, emotions, and impressions of others, and, of course, when channeled and expressed wisely; this can lead to some beautiful moments and experiences. Empaths also possess advanced levels of emotional connection and wisdom and operate at a higher emotional frequency than many. You are deeply caring and compassionate and have a big heart. Furthermore, you are in tune with psychic, subtle, and extrasensory aspects of life and expression, therefore, are often steered towards artistic, creative, and imaginative paths. Combined with your deep and unique sight, you also make incredible counselors, spiritual healers, psychics, or therapists.

Essentially, empaths possess such an advanced level of intuition and connection to others and the world that you can thrive in a number of outlets and paths. This book aims to help you 'innerstand' your unique gifts, learn how to channel them wisely and with respect to yourself with healthy boundaries, and assist in healing on all levels.

For all intents and purposes, and the power of language, 'understand' has been changed to *inner*stand throughout the rest of these chapters. When we 'innerstand' something we connect to the inner worlds and realities of being.

This book is empathic and uplifting, insightful and healing, and will hopefully leave you with a better innerstanding and integration of your unique gifts, subsequently allowing you to thrive in all aspects of life. As it is *a guide* on how to *heal psychologically and spiritually*; and use your *extraordinary gifts of intuition* among others to *survive and thrive* in the world, in these chapters, there are a series of real, down-to-earth and easily implementable self-help and development exercises, tips, and techniques to help you on your journey.

Chapter 1: Innerstanding Your Empathic Gifts and Challenges

The Empath Personality

Being an empath is a beautiful gift. You are wise and caring, insightful and perceptive. You take care of those you love and have a deep consideration and respect for all life on earth.

It is important when looking into how you can live your best life and thrive psychologically and spiritually that you first have a sound *inner*standing of what it truly means to be an empath. There are different levels to being an empath as we will explore in the next section, however, for now, let's break down the empath personality so you can innerstand it holistically.

All of the following are aspects to the empath personality however in varying degrees. For example, there may be elements you strongly resonate with and others which you only see a small part of yourself embodying. As these chapters are intended to help you *thrive* and *heal psychologically and spiritually,* it is important to explore these archetypes of yourself with an open mind and with higher awareness. This knowledge is not taught in school, nor is it widely accepted, and many unique abilities that accompany being spiritually aware and connected and existing in a higher frequency or vibrational state of being are intuitively felt and innerstood. Your empath nature connects instinctively to something beyond the everyday 'I' and often separation based reality which many people still reside in. Looking at the varying aspects to being an empath, therefore, can be a healing journey in itself.

It is OK if you only resonate with a few. Not all empaths display all of these qualities or characteristics. As you read the different aspects of the empath personality, spark your awareness back to memories or a memory where you may have been displaying some of these abilities without being conscious of what was occurring at the time. With each, there is a description of what it means, followed by how you may have been subconsciously or unconsciously displaying and embodying it.

The Artist, Creative, and Visionary

You are an artist. Due to your ability to connect to something above and beyond you through your deep and rich emotional wisdom and intuitive sight, you can also tune in to universal archetypes, ideas, concepts, and often ingenious images and thoughts in a unique way. This makes you a natural artist, creative, and visionary. Whether you choose to express yourself through song, dance, art, painting, drawing, poetry, writing, photography, film making, or directing, you can achieve great things. The visionary aspect to your nature can, literally, connect on an unseen level to some concept or archetype beyond the physical realm, and further bring it forth into the physical. Alanis Morissette is one of the most well-known empaths and even if you have not yet heard of her, her music inspires many people around the world.

Practical Implications of being the Artist, Creative and Visionary: If you embody the artist, creative, or visionary you may have found yourself as a child daydreaming and letting your mind wander to unseen worlds and ideas. Your imagination was rich and you may have been bored in social or overly externally stimulating situations. You also may have naturally had a strong inner knowing that you could come up with better or ingenious ideas and solutions to ones being presented in school, or by your teachers and peers. Your abstract and creative ways of thinking may not have been appreciated or understood by others.

The Musician, Performer, and Storyteller

Like the artist, creative and visionary, you are a musician, performer, and storyteller. Even if you don't ground this into a career or profession, you still have strong elements of being a performer. Many people naturally assume that to be an empath means to be an introvert yet they are not synergistic. Many empathic people are introverted as there are some strong intrinsic links and associations, however many empaths are also highly extroverted. This is because of your ability to connect and because of your love of connection. Once you find yourself, become centered and begin to live in an empathic and harmonious flow, you will find that using your gifts and personality strengths through poetry, performing, storyteller or by connecting others through musical expression comes naturally to you.

Practical Implications of being the Musician, the Performer, and the Storyteller: You found yourself naturally being able to play music, pick up a drum beat or understand aspects relating to advanced storytelling or performance without being taught. You had an ability to connect to others on a deep level, without teaching, and could easily and almost effortlessly pick up and adopt many roles. You may have related to characters in plays, performers, or musicians in a deeper way unexplained by your mind, and experienced certain music as a transcendental and 'other-worldly' experience.

The Dreamer, Seer, and Psychic

One thing that is not often taught in schools nor accepted mainstream is the fact that you, dear empath, are an extremely gifted person. You are a dreamer - you love to explore your dreams and merge with other worlds. Yet your abilities to merge with the subconscious also lies beyond this. Many empaths have a *seer*-like quality to them because, as stated, you can connect to some archetype or invisible symbol or idea which transcends the three-dimensional reality.

In addition to actually dreaming and enjoying the world of dreams you also may have the ability to astral travel, astral projection, or lucid dream at will. These are three things which come naturally to many empaths and when you are young you may not be able to explain them. We all have an astral body, an energetic layer of ourselves which extends beyond the physical. This astral layer of existence is responsible for all links and connections to psychic, intuitive, spiritual, and archetypal phenomena. It is also where you can connect to dream worlds and your subconscious during sleep or in that period between waking life and sleep when you are in between the worlds.

Astral travel is the ability to explore some other dimension, dream scenario or world, or altered state of consciousness at will, completely connected to your conscious mind. Astral projection is similar however instead of physically leaving your body and exploring, such as in dreams, you stay connected to your physical being and vibrate at a different frequency. Your mind is allowed to 'project' to some spiritual or multidimensional reality, usually to retrieve insight, wisdom, universal symbols and ideas, or some teachings and lessons being shown by your higher self, otherwise known as the higher mind (we will explore lucid dreaming later in this book).

Practical Implications of being the Dreamer, Seer, and the Psychic: You often had dreams you couldn't explain yet knew were sending you a message or direct insight in some way. You knew this even before reading and learning about what was occurring. If you embody these empath aspects you also have a deep inner feeling regarding people and places. You would 'just know' if somewhere didn't feel right or a person didn't have good energy. You also would know which way to go and which route was the best when on an adventure, exploration, or nature walk. Your dreams may have been vivid and you may even have found yourself become bolted out of or into your body from sleep.

The Healer, Counselor, and Therapist

Because of your unique gifts to connect to others on a deep level, you are a natural healer, counselor, and therapist. Many empaths actually go onto becoming healers, , and therapists as these paths and professions are strongly associated with your true nature. As a healer, counselor, or therapist you possess vast levels of compassion, kindness and a genuine desire to help and be of service. You have a wise and empathic nature and are very patient, and with incredible listening skills. People feel comforted, safe, and protected around you, and you tend to live and resonate in your heart chakra. Your *heart chakra* is known as the central chakra, the energy vortex which links lower self and higher self (we will look at the chakra system in detail later). It is the seat of compassion, kindness, empathy, and a connection to others and the natural world, and having a strong heart chakra enables you to thrive in any healing or counseling profession. You also may be a healer or counselor to your friends and family.

Practical Implications of being the Healer, the Counselor, and the Therapist: You had a unique way of connecting to others on a deep level and may have found strangers coming up to you to talk when in your late teens to early 20s. People had an unexplainable pull to you and knew they could open up to you. You may have had a natural connection with animals and nature and felt most content and at peace in their presence like you weren't being judged and could be yourself. You also may have been intrinsically drawn to quantum physics, eastern mythology or Buddhism books and had strong inner recognition of the significance of holistic health and alternative medicine.

The Carer, Social or Support Worker, and Companion

Connected to being a natural healer, counselor, and therapist is your inner tendencies to taking on a caring and supporting role. Many of the caregivers, social and support workers, and companions you see today are either empaths or have strong empathic tendencies. Unlike other characters and personality types, such as narcissists or energy vampires who thrive from taking from others, you thrive from giving and taking on a supportive and caring role. This is essential because of your ability and need for connection. As an empath, you are deeply connected to your environments, surroundings, and other people (and animals), and anything which threatens your connection can lead to pain, struggle, and inner turmoil. As we explore later, this is why it is essential to protect yourself and develop healthy boundaries, and why channeling and expressing these qualities of yours can lead to you living your best and most happy and harmonious life.

Practical Implications of being the Carer, the Social or Support Worker, and Companion: Growing up you may have been particularly shy and introspective and perhaps told you were too sensitive more often than not. This is because you are extremely compassionate and naturally destined to help others in some way, and take on a caring and supporting role. As a child and teenager, you may not have understood this and therefore became shy and quiet as a result. You also may have had strong feelings of wanting to be a vet or the like when asked what you want to be when you are older. Finally, you may have had a strong aversion to violence and became increasingly disturbed when seeing violent or 'hateful' acts and scenes on television or in movies, or when witnessing the suffering of others.

The Animal Whisperer, Charity Worker, and Volunteer

The empath personality is defined by connection, understanding (or now you are aware, innerstanding), and being able to feel what it is like to be another. Many empaths take this ability further and can actually read minds, or at least merge with another on such a level that they know what they are thinking or feeling. This gift can be used in *animal whispering*. You are a sensitive soul with a big heart, therefore choosing a path or career aligned to helping animals and being a guide or channel for them is a route many empaths choose to take. You tend to feel more comfortable around animals or in nature where you can just be yourself. This is where you along with many empaths not only survive but thrive. Simultaneously many empaths choose to become involved in charity or animal welfare work so this is another direction which you may share a resonance. Essentially any hobby, career, path or direction allowing you to make use of your sensitive, caring, empathic and intuitive gifts will allow you to shine.

Practical Implications of being the Animal Whisperer, Charity Worker, and Volunteer: You may have developed a deep and personal relationship to animals which no one knew about. When visiting zoos, sanctuaries, wildlife areas or parks you could speak to animals on an inner level and felt an emotional and telepathic connection. When coming across a homeless person in the street you have had real and sincere compassion for them, which sometimes translated into pain. You may have also felt different from your family in some unexplainable way.

The Tarot Reader, Spiritual Healer, and Energy Worker

This brings us on to the spiritual stuff. You are deeply spiritual and intuitive, even if you are not yet conscious of it. This can manifest in many 'magical' ways such as knowing what someone is about to say before they say it, sensing an event about to occur, or being able to pull something out of someone hidden deep within. You may be psychic, have precognitive dreams or even visions and may live in an alternate reality together. Many empaths exist in multiple dimensions with one foot in this world and the other in another. This allows you to connect with a higher source or power. Whether you call this god, the goddess, spirit, or the universe, it is very real to you, and when *tuning in* to connect to these realms you can be a powerful and unique asset in someone's life. You may use your spiritual gifts and awareness to write books, heal others, teach in some way or take on a leadership role. Mother Teresa is a prime example of a spiritual empath who used her gifts in service to others.

Practical Implications of being the Tarot Reader, Spiritual Healer, and Energy Worker: You were deeply drawn to all thing mystical, spiritual and metaphysical from your mid to late teens. You may have been interested in quantum physics, crystals, astrology, supernatural abilities, and ancient wisdom. You possessed a deep knowing of all things and could see beyond people's hidden motives, feelings, and intentions. You may have begun meditating at a young age, and reading spiritual literature or wisdom infused books on the occult, spiritual or metaphysical topics. Your dreams may have been vast and profound and you may have naturally begun to astral project or lucid dream. All of your senses become heightened and your love for animals and mother earth increased with the more knowledge you acquired.

The Independent Worker and 'Self-Employed One'

Because of your inherent dislike of certain characters, roles, interactions, and energies you are most suited to self-employment or highly independent roles. This can manifest in a number of ways such as through being a self-employed plumber, electrician, handywoman or man or owning your own small business. The main point with this is that you have an aversion and furthermore extreme sensitivity to certain noises which come with 'normal' jobs. Working in an office, for example, can be extremely stressful and even harmful to your empathic nature, as can working in sales or any job where you have to interact with a large number of people on a daily basis.

Practical Implications of being the Independent Worker and Self-Employed One: You had a particular aversion in school to certain topics and perspectives taught as truth. You were not necessarily an outward rebel but you were an inward one, and frequently went against the norm. Structure and oppressive ways made you feel limited and you preferred to come up with your own creative solutions and ways of thinking than following set orders. Rules and regulations may have seemed oppressive to you and your political views may have been strongly steered towards liberalism.

Although these are not the different types of empath becoming aware of the varying aspects to the empath personality and your nature can really aid in your journey of discovery and self- development. Empathy is an encompassing gift and its applications are vast. Inner and understanding yourself may just be the key to your own personal puzzle!

The Different Types of Empath

Technically speaking, there are not different 'types' of empaths, however more varying elements and degrees of being an empath. In this section, therefore, we will explore the different types or varying degrees of the empath personality with the intention of self-discovery and *inner*standing. As you read them, you may find that many resonate and overlap as 'being an empath' is a holistic experience.

Emotional Empaths

Emotional empaths are the most common and well-known types of empaths. To be an empath is to be able to connect with others on an emotional level. Emotional empaths, therefore, can tune in and merge with another and are able to feel their emotions as their own. If expressed positively, you can use this as a great gift, being a guiding light and wayshower through advanced and mature levels of emotional wisdom and expression. If, however, you have not yet learned how to stay centered and grounded and protect yourself from potentially harmful influences, this can have some seriously detrimental effects. You can absorb other people's moods and emotions to the point of being sad, hurt, confused, in pain or depressed, and often you won't even know why. In this sense you act as an *emotional sponge*, taking on every feeling and thought which accompanies as your own.

When mastered, of course, this emotional sensitivity can be used as a gift, and can also be used to get to the bottom of deceitful or ill-intentioned people to know what they are hiding.

Intellectual Empaths

These types of empaths are often not widely known due to naturally associating empathy with emotions and intuition. Intellectual empaths, however, possess a unique gift in that they are able to speak and communicate in a rare way. You can merge with another's mind or energy body and come up with information, wisdom, words, and phrases which are not known to your conscious mind. For example, if you are an intellectual empath, you may have once read something in a book or heard a piece of information which then becomes stored in the subconscious. When you next interact with someone some subtle energy triggers your mind into knowing about some seriously complex topics. *Mirroring* behavior, intellect, and mind comes naturally therefore and often leaves you with an *i*nner knowing and shock simultaneously, along with the lines of 'how did I know this,' or 'wow- I'm a genius!'

You can also adapt your vocabulary, speech, and style to different people from all sorts of backgrounds.

Intuitive Empaths

If you are an intuitive empath, you embody an element of all the different types of empaths. Intuition is a gift which defines the personality and nature of an empath as intuition is the ability to be in tune with your senses. When you intuit something you feel or sense what is about to happen. When you are connected to your intuition, you are connected to your place of knowing and power. Being intuitive, therefore, leads to all the other unique aspects and types of empathy. This advanced intuition can be used as a gift, such as in healing, psychic or spiritual phenomena, helping others or animals, or through counseling.

Psychic or Medical Empaths

Psychic or medical empaths take on the physical ailments of others. Like an emotional empath who absorbs the emotions of others, psychic or medical empaths pick up on the physical state and energy of other people's bodies. This can present itself in many ways such as through physically taking on the symptoms, aches, and pains of another. For example, feeling like you have a pain in your leg when someone else has a pain in their leg or briefly getting headache symptoms when near someone with a headache; or by sensing the energetic and physical state of another. You may *just know* that someone has a stomach ache or is going through a painful moon cycle (period), or perhaps is dealing with a toothache. This is because you are connected to many dimensions including the subtle and spiritual therefore you sense things above and beyond the norm.

Many psychic empaths go on to become healers of some sort due to this special gift including therapists, physicians, massage therapists, reflexologists, aromatherapists, energy workers or bodyworkers. Some empaths can even *see* energy blockages in another directly!

Spiritual Empaths

Spiritual empaths are essentially the natural mediums, psychics, clairvoyants, and 'channels.' You can act as a channel for many things and aspects of consciousness and higher awareness to shine through such as by connecting to the spirit or some 'subtle-energetic' thought form. If you are a spiritual empath, you have the ability to not only communicate with the spirit or some higher power but to also *feel* the emotional, mental, and physical (medical) state of another person, animal or natural entity. You are like emotional and psychic/medical empaths, but with a more holistic and encompassing understanding.

Many spiritual empaths go on to become great healers, spiritual teachers or guides as you can, literally, tune in and connect to any body, dimension, frequency or subtle state of existence. There is always some genuine desire to do good and be of service and never to harm or exert an unhealthy and boastful ego. You may also be clairvoyant, clairsentient, and clairaudient, therefore, sense, feel, and hear things from other dimensions.

Animal Empaths

As an animal empath, you possess the unique gift to communicate and connect with animals on a deep and rare level. This can be expressed through animal whispering as mentioned earlier or you may evolve this gift into simply becoming more mindful and present with it. Many animal empaths feel more connected and comfortable around the presence of animals (as opposed to being around humans), and animals sense this. There is an underlying feeling of 'magic' when connected to an animal, such as a horse, dog or cat, in an empathic way, and the animals too sense the intentions and awareness of the empath. Even if you do not necessarily consider yourself an animal communicator or whisperer connecting to this aspect of yourself can enhance your life greatly, and increase your confidence in your abilities simultaneously.

Plant Empaths

You are intrinsically connected to the plants, trees, flowers, and natural entities of the world. Like an emotional empath who can tune into others' emotions, you have a unique ability to connect to plants on a deep level. You have a natural intuition about what plants and flowers need and may not have ever read a specialist book on how to grow, care or maintain special plants. Simultaneously you may find that seeds and flowers grow and thrive in your presence. This is due to your *aura* and the intentions you subtly exhibit. Plants, like people and animals, respond to energy and subtle impressions, and many plant empaths make great shamans and healers due to the ability to feel the spirit on the plant queen and kingdoms.

If you are a plant empath you may walk into a friend or family member's home and instantly know that the plant may need fresh water or may be wanting to be moved to a different location. Furthermore, you can actually receive guidance from trees and flowers and communicate on a telepathic level!

Environmental Empaths

As an environmental empath, you have a fine-tuned sense to the natural wonders of the earth. You can sense and 'read' physical locations, natural objects, and places of energetic significance. Sacred sites have a special resonance to you and you may be able to feel things beyond the physical senses from stepping into a place, for example, a holy site, a temple on sacred grounds, or places like Stonehenge. Environmental empaths are also known as *geometric* empaths due to the geographical element of their gifts. Natural objects such as gemstones, crystals, and rocks can be connected with to receive information, and you can sense and feel other people's emotions, memories, and experiences when stepping into a place.

When honed and developed environmental empaths can use their abilities like a compass, tuning into the physical and environmental locations for all sorts of extrasensory experiences and wisdom to come through. It is also important as an environmental empath to spend time in nature as you often need to 'recharge' due to your heightened sensitivity to external influence.

Introverted Empaths

Introverted empaths are the type of empaths many people mistake the empath personality for. Being an empath is not synergistic with being introverted, however, they are linked. Introverts are people who feel more comfortable in the inner worlds of being and subsequently enjoy activities like reading, journaling, introspection, gaming, gardening, and solitude over any extroverted or loud activities and interactions. As empaths generally prefer one to one or more intimate, authentic, and real conversation and connection, if you resonate with this type of empath personality then you display the qualities of an introvert. You do not necessarily inherently dislike social situations and are not 'not extrovert,' however, you do have an aversion of some sort to overly loud and domineering characters and busy social scenarios.

As an introverted empath, you can use your love of solitude, one-to-one or smaller interactions and introspective activities to develop your empathic nature and gifts further.

Activist Empaths

Activist empaths can also be called 'the warrior- empath.' This is because, quite simply, you are a warrior and an activist and stand up for what you believe in. You use your empathic gifts and unique perceptive insight and intuition to help others in some way whether that be an activist for animals, other people, or the environment. Activist empaths have a sense of mission or purpose and are always strong, bold, courageous, and fearless, therefore making compassionate and powerful leaders. You still take time to recharge and connect to your inner source of power, but you are also strong in your beliefs and convictions and harness your empathy to do good in the world.

Many activist empaths go on to become campaigners, politicians, leaders, or speakers or may choose to channel their abilities in some creative or artistic field with a big vision.

As you can see from the descriptions there are many types of an empath. All fundamentally share the same unique quality which allows for your unique insight and perception. This gift is *intuition*.

In the rest of these chapters we will explore real techniques and methods to ground and develop your intuition, and other special qualities, so you can live the life you deserve.

The Science of Empathy

As you are aware by now, an empath is someone who is able to connect with others on a deep level. You may feel their feelings, share their emotions, and take them on as if they are your own; or read their minds. You sense things far beyond 'the norm' and can relate to animals, plants, and nature in a unique and often *extra*ordinary way.

So how does this measure scientifically?

Everything has a scientific basis just as everything is spiritual. Energetic laws govern the physical world we reside in and the term *spirit science* is arguably one of the most accurate ways to measure and define empathy and the gifts that come with it. Being an empath is a real and sincere journey. There are no 'boxes' or superficial components to your life, and you live from the heart in an interconnected way. Real values such as compassion, kindness, living with heart and, of course, empathy, reside and take central significance over any cynicism, false motives or intentions, or cold and harsh realities. In this respect, attempting to measure or define who you are and your nature can almost be seen as pointless.

Due to the fact that many of the techniques and routes to healing psychologically and spiritually do require some scientific understanding and innerstanding, we will briefly explore the science of empathy. Some of it is pretty fascinating!

Let's look at a few key scientific angles to help you *inner*stand your empathy.

Neurological Activity and Neuroscience

The human brain is essentially governed by neurons connected and interacting on an intrinsic level. Neurons are responsible for all thoughts, feelings, beliefs, and responses to internal and external stimuli. Together they make a 'web' like structure, with each individual neuron responsible for the rest. In terms of being an empath, possessing feelings such as compassion, kindness, and empathy all reflect on neurological activity in the brain, thus affecting the empath's responses and feelings to certain situations.

In *Psychology Today,* Judith Orloff M.D, author of 'The Empath's Survival Guide,' goes on to suggest that empaths have *a mirror neuron system*. In other words, *you mirror other people's neurons*. Researchers have further discovered that the brain consists of a specialized group of neurons responsible for compassion which allow us to mirror and share in people's pain, happiness, sadness and joy (and many other emotions and states of being). As an empath, you have hyper-responsive neurons, unlike narcissists and certain socio and psychopathic personalities and characters who have *underactive* neurological responses, therefore you experience other people's emotions on an inner and neurological level.

Essentially neuroscience has paved a way for new ways of thinking and understanding (and innerstanding) empathy and furthermore steps to healing and self-help which accompany each other. The brain is a powerful thing, yet it is only a vessel and tool for consciousness. As an empath, you exhibit far advanced levels of consciousness, awareness, and intuition based on your connection to others. Spiritually, one can call this energy or *being energetically connected on a deeper level*; scientifically we can refer to the knowledge that you mirror neurons.

Electromagnetic Energy Fields

All of life on earth contains an electromagnetic energy field. This energy field is responsible for picking up, receiving and transmitting information, sensory stimuli and information and simultaneously interacts on a subtle level with all other energy fields. All living organisms have an electromagnetic field including us and natural entities such as plants, trees, and gemstones. In science, this energy field is known as the electromagnetic field however to many aware of our spiritual essence and the spiritual aspects to reality this is known as the *aura*. The aura and the electromagnetic field essentially serve the same function. They both allow for the transmission of thought, feeling, emotion, and sensory information, however, the only difference is arguably the function scientists and spiritualists give them.

It is in this space - the aura or electromagnetic energy field, where empaths can suffer most harm or alternatively survive and thrive. Due to being so susceptible to the emotions and feelings of others and other people's intentions, whether positive and helpful or negative and harmful, an unbounded or unprotected aura energy field can have some serious effects. As we will explore in depth later it is essential as an empath to learn how to protect your energy and stay *grounded, centered, and aligned* to your true self, truth and empathic nature.

In *Psychology Today*, Judith Orloff M.D goes on to say "According to the HeartMath Institute, these fields transmit information about people's thoughts and emotions. Empaths may be particularly sensitive to this input and tend to become overwhelmed by it. Similarly, we often have stronger physical and emotional responses to changes in the electromagnetic fields of the earth and sun. Empaths know well that what happens to the earth and sun affects our state of mind and energy."[1]

---

[1] https://www.psychologytoday.com/gb/blog/the-empaths-survival-guide/201703/the-science-behind-empathy-and-empaths

Dopamine and Synesthesia

As you may already know, dopamine is the neurotransmitter responsible for all feel-good and happy feelings. It is also possibly one of the most profound truths which help explain the scientific nature of an empath. Research has found that introverted empaths have a higher sensitivity to dopamine than extroverts. This means that introverted empaths need less external stimuli or interaction to feel happy and receive the pleasure response (associated with dopamine). You can essentially *feel good from your own inner being.*

In terms of being an empath, this is fascinating! It means you have the ability to thrive from your own inner levels of being. Activities which many empaths enjoy due to your love of depth and connection including reading, journaling, connecting with animals, and nature; being a good friend in need or helping others and spending time alone to introspect or recharge - can all trigger dopamine and the feel-good factor. To help innerstand this better is the fact that non-empathic people may need some overly dominant and extroverted activity or situation to make them feel good.

Finally, synesthesia is something which can be used to help innerstand the nature of being an empath. Synesthesia is the ability to see colors upon hearing a specific piece of music or *tasting* words, thoughts, or mental projections. It is essentially the neurological pairing of two different senses in the brain. According to *Psychology Today*, mirror-touch synesthesia - as displayed by empaths - is the ability to feel the emotions and sensations of others in your own body, as if they are your own.

Empath Struggles

You are all too familiar with the struggles that come with being an empath. Growing up, you may have been called 'too sensitive,' labeled as shy and introspective, or even taunted, bullied, or teased because of it. You may have been brought up in oppressive structures or regimes contrary to your empathic nature and you might have simply been misunderstood and overlooked. Your unique gifts and abilities may not have been seen or appreciated due to growing up in a masculine and extroverted world.

This brings us onto *The Wound of the Soul*. It is important when exploring how to heal psychology and spiritually that we look to the subconscious and real-life factors which shape the empathic journey. *The Wound of the Soul* can be split into two distinct parts: **Childhood Wounds** and **The Shadow Self.**

Let's look at these now.

Childhood Wounds

As a child, you were often told you were too sensitive, needed to toughen up or shamed in some way for your sensitivities. This created an *inner wound* which you brought into adult life. We all carry wounds, as we are all human. Wounds and traumas are part of the human experience. However this specific wound is linked to being an empath, and more specifically showing beautiful empathic displays.

It all comes down to society, patriarchy and the existing structures in play. Empathy can arguably be seen as a feminine quality due to its link to introspection, feeling and emotion, and often introversion. Those of us who are highly empathic are often said to be predominantly *yin*. Yin is the opposite of yang, yet together they make a whole - a unified energetic state. Yin and yang are the opposing yet complementary forces of the universe. Every living thing contains yin and yang as they are the magnetic and electric forces (aspects) of the physical world.

We won't go into yin and yang in too much detail here, however, for now; it is important to recognize that empaths are predominantly yin as they are more connected to their emotions. Emotions are a yin and 'watery' quality. As society is mainly yang - fiery, extroverted, masculine (patriarchal) and mind based, this is can, therefore, be difficult for a young empath.

In school, the norm is to be loud, confident, expressive and work rationally and logically. Being artistic, creative and intuitive are almost seen as some 'extracurricular' activity, as if they are separate to society in some way. Yet, anyone who has studied psychology and the biological and neurological aspects to both the brain and self, know that we are not just rational and reasonable creatures. Reason, rationality, and logic are essential, yet we also have a right brain - a *right hemisphere* responsible for intuition, music, creativity, and original thought. Many empaths are balanced but also tend to think and perceive from 'a right brain way of thinking.'

So growing up you may not have been appreciated or seen for your unique ways of seeing. Your creative and artistic gifts may have been overlooked and you may not have been given the encouragement and support you needed to thrive and develop your inner gifts further. In addition, you may have suffered ill-treatment if you were a shy, introverted or introspective empath, in the form of teasing, bullying, or shaming in some way.

Essentially, you were like a fish out of water.

As you know empathy is defined by a rich imagination, advanced emotional wisdom and connection, and a tendency towards deep, authentic, and real connection. As an empath, you may thrive in solo activities or one-to-one communications, and you may enjoy the introspective activities as described earlier like gaming, gardening, reading, spending time in nature, or expressing yourself in solitude through art or music. You also may be an original thinker, a philosopher at heart, or possess a deeply inventive and creative mind. Finally, you may have had a sense of spiritual knowing and were drawn to unexplainable phenomena. All of these can be suppressed and even ridiculed in western society.

Because children require the support, care, wisdom, and guidance from grown-ups, not having the support or encouragement necessary as an empath inevitably created wounds within. To some, they are only minor and allow the adult empath to function and experience daily life like any other adult, yet to others, these wounds can run deep, and because the ways of the empath are not taught or even widely accepted, they never heal these wounds.

Luckily, you have books like *Intuitive Empath*, so you will be just fine!

The Shadow Self

This brings us on to the shadow self. The shadow is linked to childhood wounds as it is part of yourself that you have hidden, suppressed, or rejected, however, it is different as it is associated with *the collective*. Unlike childhood wounds, which are a direct result of upbringing and external influences and environments, the shadow self is part of the collective psyche and consciousness.

Exploring your shadow can be an extremely helpful and beneficial tool for psychological and spiritual growth and healing. The famous psychiatrist and one of the founding fathers of modern psychology, Carl Jung, came up with a set of *universal archetypes* to define the whole self. These universal archetypes are inherent within all human beings and often appear as symbols in dreams. *The shadow* is one of the fundamental components to Carl Jung's archetypes and something you can build a relationship with to begin to recognize parts of yourself you may be hiding, rejecting, or repressing altogether.

Let's briefly look at some of the shadow aspects to being an empath.

- **Lack of Self-Love.** This is due to your attempt to be 'everyone's empath' or the shoulder to cry on. In your attempt to always be there for someone else, you often neglect your own needs. This can lead to depleted energy and, eventually, if left unhealed and over a long period of time, inner resentments and feelings of being used.

- ***Suppression of Intimacy and Connection.*** Despite your innate longing for connection and depth one of the main shadow aspects to being an empath is not being able to open up to intimacy and connection, whether romantic or platonic. This is due to how intensely you feel and experience life. Simply put, sometimes it can be too hard to open up fully and merge with someone on a real level because you know how much it will hurt if the bond were to ever break.

- ***Suppression of Sex and Desire.*** Linking with suppression of intimacy and connection is the suppression of sex and desire. This shadow element is actually one of the main collective shadow aspects to human nature and the self and is one of the things that is widely taught in Jung's school of thought. The human experience involves desire and primal passion, yet we reject and deny this aspect of self due to some misperception that it is 'unpure' or dirty in some way. This distorted beliefs ultimately leads to many of the problems and imbalances we see in the world regarding sexuality and specifically, in empath sexual relationships. We will explore sexual relationships in depth later.

- ***The Simple Life.*** One minor aspect to the empath shadow is the denial and rejection of materialism and living an abundant and prosperous life. This is not always the case however there are some empaths who hold this truth. Because empathy is defined and characterized by a strong *spiritual awareness,* and connection to something beyond the everyday 'I' and ego reality, there are empaths who feel they are not worthy of financial bliss. This ultimately leaves you in a state of suffering, repression, and imbalance, as abundance is your birthright. Taking steps to heal your relationship with money can really aid in finding your flow and living your best life.

- ***Suppression of Success.*** Again, you may suffer from the belief that you are not allowed to achieve success and must live your life in service to some person, animal or cause. Selflessness is a beautiful quality to possess and is one of your positive qualities (your 'light'), yet when taken too far this can lead to unhealthy selflessness and selfishness on yourself. Many empaths suffer from feeling like they must give but not receive. Life is supposed to be a healthy flow of giving and receiving and personal successes, joys and pleasures should be embraced. This empath shadow aspect can be overcome through developing self-esteem and self-worth and through creating better boundaries.

- ***Blocks to Health and Self- Mastery.*** A shadow aspect to empathy is having an innate block to self- care and health. It is not that you don't want to be whole, healed and thrive, it is just that you are so busy taking care of everyone and everything else - even if just in your mind and your emotions - that you prevent yourself from living *your* best life. Self-mastery is a very important part of being an empath as your unique gifts cannot shine when you are depleted in other areas. Your deep and advanced emotional connection, profound intuitive and often spiritual and psychic sight, and unique cognitive and mental functioning cannot maintain their levels if other parts of yourself are neglected. In the final section of this book, we look at self-mastery and how to attain it.

- **Solitude.** Many empaths have a deep and sometimes dark desire for solitude. Solitude and taking time to recharge your energy is natural, however, the 'darkness' comes when you begin to feel negative emotions at the thought of being in a social situation or gathering. Insecurity, fear, anxiety, stress, or nervous tension are all aspects which may arise when spending too much time in solitude, to the point that it can actually become a part of you (hence why it is referred to here in *the shadow*). Solitude is often seen in many introverts, therefore, working on embodying more *extroverted characteristics* can really help transcend this need for solitude.

- **Escapism**. Linking with solitude is escapism. As an empath, who feels the pain of the world and all sentient life's sufferings, escaping from the harsh realities is an integral element to your personality. Of course, not all empaths do resort to escapism, however, you are prone to it and when you do it can have some seriously detrimental consequences. It can lead to addictions, which we explore in the next point.

- **Addictions.** For an empath, addictions can manifest in many ways. Food, tobacco, drugs, sex, porn, substance, television; these are all outlets an empath may turn to. Over time these become integrated into your personality and actively begin to restructure and reshape your DNA. This is why it is important to take steps to heal early on, and why connecting to your unique gifts and empathic abilities can help you turn away this shadow aspect of self.

- **Victim-Martyr-Savior.** Finally, the victim-martyr-savior complex is a very prominent aspect to the shadow side of an empath. This refers to the feeling of being a victim followed by believing one needs to take on martyrdom or a savior role. This is a vicious cycle which leaves the poor empath in a state of suffering, trauma, and victimhood drained of their energy and unable to step fully into their true power. It can be very easy to feel and even take on the role of a victim, especially when often dealing with narcissists, energy vampires, and other toxic personalities (until you learn how to block them and put up better boundaries).

So instead of turning towards self-development, self-healing, and self-love and care many empaths turn towards sacrifice, martyrdom, or saviorhood. Recognizing this aspect of self is the first step to healing it!

Other struggles which are not necessarily aspects of the shadow self or personality, however, do present themselves often, are self-consciousness and inability to speak your truth, self-esteem and self-worth issues, fear of public spaces, and oversensitivity in intimate relationships.

The Wound of the Soul

The wound of the soul is the part of self which is carried throughout lifetimes. This means that you have experienced many lifetimes wherein each, you have brought lessons with you into the next. You finally reach your current stage of evolution and self-awareness in this life with all of the lessons and teachings as a part of your unique *soulprint*.

As an empath, this means that you have already gone through many tests, trails, and learnings which have resulted in you being able to vibrate and experience life in your current resonance. All of life involves resonance and vibration as all of life involves frequency. We are magnetic, electric, biological, and energetic beings, and our cells hold memories stored in our DNA. Through certain practices, these memories can be activated and parts of our DNA which were once dormant can too be activated.

Although it may seem 'deep' and complex, many of the daily struggles you face as an empath can be traced back to soul wounds which, when *inner*stood, is not that complex.

If you look at life like layers, *multidimensionality* is not really that hard to innerstand. You have a mental body (a mind), an emotional body (emotions), a physical body (your body), a spiritual body (spirit), and an astral or energetic body (your aura). There are also other subtle levels of reality and being but these are mainly shared by various thinkers and teachers through direct experience and ancient texts. The wound of the soul, therefore, can be seen as your *holistic journey* and collective experience throughout both this lifetime and many.

There have been many in-depth books written on DNA, soulprints, and multidimensional living, however, the main point is always to innerstand how you can heal, survive and thrive in this life. Being *aware* of your soul's unique journey is a fundamental aspect of this.

Chapter 2: How to Manage Your Energy

Innerstanding What is Yours

One of the main struggles with being an empath is taking on all that is not yours. Thoughts, emotions, wounds, feelings, and impressions all become absorbed through your energy body. This can be highly detrimental to yourself and if left unchecked can lead to repetitive cycles, low moods, and states of suffering.

It is natural as an empath to want to heal and help others - it is simply your nature. Yet when taken to extremes this desire to help others ultimately creates a paradox in which you find yourself suffering from no energy and physically, mentally, emotionally, and spiritually feeling drained. This is especially true with narcissists and energy vampires. To counter this, therefore, and bring some much needed surviving and thriving energy back into your life, there are specific exercises, techniques, and activities you can engage in daily to re-*energize* and re-*center*.

We cover some of these in detail throughout the rest of the book so for now, let's look at these at face value to pave the way.

- **Nature.** Connecting to nature can aid greatly in your ability to re-energize and recharge yourself.
- **Chakras**. Learning about your chakras and becoming knowledgeable of the inner energies at play will allow you to heal yourself on all levels, and also be aware of what may be going on behind the scenes.
- **Aura Strengthening and Protecting Exercises**. Engaging in exercises that can strengthen and protect your aura can really help you to not only survive but thrive, in your empathic gifts and life.
- **Meditation and Mindfulness**. Incorporating meditation and mindfulness into a daily routine will allow you to develop stronger inner boundaries, a stronger sense of intuition and more confidence and self-esteem. They will also increase your unique empathic gifts.
- **Sound and Mantras:** Introducing sound therapy or healing and mantras can re-shape, re-structure and rewire the neurons in your brain to deal with any

potential struggles that come with being an empath, while simultaneously allowing for new ways of thinking and perceiving, and enhancing any psychic or spiritual gifts.

- ***Psychology and 'the Self:'*** Exploring psychology and the Self enable you to learn about the shadow or 'dark side' of being an empath, so you can bring shadow aspects of yourself to light.
- ***Journalling and Dream Diary***: Journalling and beginning a dream diary will allow you to keep a record of your emotions, memories, experience, and learnings to enable you to thrive as an empath. A Dream diary or journal can have a profound effect on waking life through the subconscious messages, symbols, and teachings shown in dreams.

The Importance of Boundaries and Grounding

Boundaries is your new power word. Being an empath is hard, what with your heightened sensitivity and higher frequency emotional connection and functioning. One of your main issues in life, therefore, is to develop and make friends with the word boundaries. It may be difficult at first, especially due to your innate desire to be 'everyone's friend in need' and help others in some way, yet, as you know, this leaves you drained and lacking in energy, vitality, and wellbeing.

One of the key pieces of wisdom to be aware of when learning about your boundaries is the recent discoveries of neuroscience and quantum physics. Neuroscientists and quantum physicists have found that we are in fact governed by an aura, an electromagnetic energy field which emits, transmits, and receives thoughts, emotions, and subtle impressions. Our auras - or electromagnetic fields - interact with others yet this is not just limited to other humans. Every living thing from plants to flowers and crystals or rocks have an auric field. This means we essentially *converse* with others on a subtle level in every moment of now.

Now, this has some profound implications. Emotions, subtle energy, and unique spiritual-energetic gifts define empathy, therefore being aware of the power of your own being can be heaven or hell- literally. This is where boundaries come into play.

As you will see later narcissists and other toxic personalities are magnets to your vibe. They simply love your energy, love, compassion, and inner beauty but not in a healthy way. This means that having healthy boundaries and centeredness is essential.

Fortunately, there are many ways to do this. We go through these in the next section.

How to Protect your Energy: Techniques and Exercises!

In this section, you will find a rich and detailed account of various methods and techniques to protect, enhance, and develop your energy. Many of them interlink with other chapters and sections throughout the book, so hopefully, these will act as your guide and compass for the rest of your days!

In this section we explore:

- Self-love
- The healing power of special gemstones and crystals
- Meditation
- The power of chi and chi balls
- Psychic Awareness
- Aura Protection
- Grounding/tree meditation
- Self-hypnosis

Visualization, meditation, mindfulness, chi and energy, colors, nature and the elements, yin and yang, psychic strengthening, hands-on healing/energy healing.

Aura protection exercises

One of the most powerful (and loving) things you could do for yourself is to protect your aura. To some, these techniques may seem slightly 'woo' but spirituality and metaphysics are a fundamental part of life. Many of the people who are living their dream lives, healthy, abundant, and happy with a strong inner focus and protection and genuine love for life are those who are in tune with their spirituality. Aura protection exercises, therefore, will steer you effectively on the journey to healing and wholeness - any overcoming and sabotaging or destructive thoughts or behaviors.

- **Work with Crystals.** Crystals embody certain energetic frequencies which can interact with our energy fields for a desired effect. Crystals, therefore, are extremely powerful when wishing to strengthen your aura, protect yourself and develop healthy boundaries. Let's look at three main crystals which can help you in everyday life.

Black Tourmaline: Black tourmaline is specifically referred to as the protection stone. It is grounding, provides a sense of security and trust, and shields you from any 'dark,' harmful, or negative energy. Connecting to this stone can help you feel stronger inside and increase a sense of confidence. Meditating with, connecting to, and simply wearing a black tourmaline bracelet, pendant, or necklace will literally 'shield' you from unwanted energy and interaction (just remember that we use quartz crystals to power watches!).

Amethyst: Amethyst is particularly effective in protecting your aura as it increases your sense of intuition and *inner knowing*. Amethyst is purple and has a majestic feel. It, therefore, can enhance your perception, connect you to your higher mind and inner knowing, and aid in mental clarity in strength when dealing with unsavory characters or situations. Amethyst can act as a psychic shield against negative or harmful energy, therefore, protecting yourself. Again, this crystal can be worn as jewelry or carried around as an individual stone.

Hematite: Hematite is another grounding stone as is helps absorb negative energy and protect your energy field. It can enhance confidence, increase your ability to transform negative situations into positive ones and can calm the mind when responding to stress, anxiety, or worry. Hematite also has an effect on the physical body by its electromagnetic effect on the cells. It can aid in detoxification and strengthen the liver and blood, therefore, enabling you to better protect yourself. Hematite can be carried around and held and connected to for protection and strength in destructive situations.

(There is a crystal meditation at the end of this chapter!)

- **Self-hypnosis.** Self-hypnosis is similar with working with crystals in that your magnetic energy field is strengthened and protected, however, with self-hypnosis, it is your mind having a direct effect as opposed to crystals. You can literally rewire and restructure your mind (through neurological activity, belief, and thought patterns and reconditioning) which can then act as a tool to shield you from harmful energy. Everything can be seen to start in the mind as the mind is the root of all problems, concerns, solutions, and manifestations of recovery.

Self-hypnosis can be performed through many means such as mental reprogramming, mantras, meditation, focused mindfulness, sound therapy, binaural beats and music, reiki and energy healing, and making a conscious effort daily to realign your thoughts and inner focus. You can also see a professional hypnotherapist and gain insights and directions through someone experienced in their field. The key is to remember the power of your mind and to be aware of any unconscious or subconscious beliefs that may be limiting your perspective and holding you down. Once these perspectives are released, your ability to protect yourself through the mind, intention, and thought alone will become clear and amplified. You can also amplify your empathic gifts through the connection self-hypnosis brings to the subconscious.

- **Connect with nature.** Connecting with nature is possibly one of the most effective ways to protect yourself and strengthen your inner boundaries. Nature connects us to all that is, expands our minds, brings mental focus and clarity, heals emotions, releases wounds and traumas, increases our sense of self and therefore confidence, and generally leads to an enhanced and improved way of being. Developing a special relationship with the elements can really help in your ability to remain strong and centered within and to put up better boundaries.

Try the tree meditation below to help center and ground yourself. You will find that your power to protect yourself in harmful situations and ground your sensitivities will be amplified immensely!

Tree meditation for inner grounding

Visit your favorite nature spot or a local park or field. Find somewhere quiet or somewhere you feel comfortable. Find a tree with strong roots and a big trunk and sit down with your back straight gently resting against the trunk and your knees bent with your feet on the ground. It is best to perform this barefoot as being barefoot grounds your energy with the earth. (Think of chi and life force!)

Close your eyes and focus on your breath. Take note of all the sensations around you, the sounds, smells (hopefully of nature), physical sensations and your connection to this strong and ancient tree. Bring your awareness within while still remaining conscious of your surroundings. Once you are calm, peaceful and centered within with an acute awareness of both your physical body and surroundings, try this.

- As you breathe in, visualize a white or golden light being equated with your breath. Watch it travel up your body from your feet to the top of your head and back down again. Do this for 8-10 deep breaths until you feel it starts to come naturally.

- Next, visualize that same white or golden light traveling up the trunk of the tree,

- from its roots all the way up to the top of its leaves and back down again. Visualize this happening to the tree as you breathe.

- Finally, synchronize your breath, the visualization of energy traveling through and up yourself and back down again, and the visualization of energy traveling up the tree from the roots to leaves and back down into the earth into one. Merge the individual parts into *synergy* and feel the energy flow through both you and the tree as one.

This exercise is very powerful for grounding yourself, gaining inner strength and chi and protecting your energy. The effects can be used in a number of circumstances and specifically, will aid in how you respond to and interact with toxic people, use your empathic and intuitive gifts, and regain your confidence psychologically and spiritually.

Crystal Meditation/Connecting to Special Gemstones

Crystals have been used by ancient cultures for thousands of years. As a crystal is formed directly from the earth with thousands of years of celestial energy and planetary projections, each gemstone embodies a certain frequency and vibrational quality. We can, therefore, connect and tune in to crystals to receive their healing power!

As this exercise is intended to connect to crystals for *aura-strengthening and protecting* purposes, here are the main crystals I would recommend purchasing:

- Amethyst: Reminder: Amethyst is particularly powerful for your third eye, the brow chakra which relates to all psychic phenomena, extra-sensory perception and awareness, dream states, and enhanced intuition. It helps with protection as it expands awareness, increasing your ability to sense energy and enhances your mental powers of auric-field protection and inner-chi strength.

- Quartz: This gem embodies 'white light,' the purest frequency and a blank canvas for your intentions. This crystal can be programmed with any intention and element to develop the desired effect. If you wish for strength, you can program the crystal with strength. If you need more mental clarity and confidence in speaking your truth or putting up better boundaries, this can be achieved. Any empathic quality or unique ability which corresponds can be amplified. Quartz crystal is a clear canvas.

- Black Tourmaline: Reminder: this crystal is specifically known as the protecting and aura-strengthening stone. It embodies a grounding and stabilizing energy and is particularly effective as it encompasses you in a psychic shield which can be integrated into daily life. Black tourmaline raises your vibration and can act as a sponge against dark, harmful, or detrimental energies.

The Meditation:

First, it is essential to cleanse and charge your crystal. This is because crystals absorb the energies of others, so cleansing it in water and recharging it in direct sunlight are the best ways to see results.

Create a sacred space, such as with incense, burning oils, frankincense or sage, and either peaceful meditation music, nature sounds, or binaural beats. Get comfortable and hold the crystal in the palm of your left hand with your right hand hovering over the top. Begin your breathing and go within, feeling both your own energy and the crystal's.

Feel into this space for a while and focus your intention on enhancing, expanding, and filling this special gem with light and the frequency you wish to embody. Essentially, fill the crystal up with the quality. Once you have begun to feel a swirl of chi (universal life force energy), you can expand your intentions.

The key with this exercise is to focus on your intention—what exactly you wish to charge the crystal with, your breath and inner state, and the harmonious and synergistic relationship between your own energy field and the crystal's. With practice, it will be very easy to connect to the gemstone's energy field and tune in effortlessly for healing, wholeness and integration, and protection. Remember, it is essential that your crystals are cleansed and recharged.

You can also carry black tourmaline around with you as it is the psychic-shield and energy-field protecting stone. The same applies for Amethyst if you wish to stay connected to your intuitive and psychic powers!

Creating a Chi Ball

Creating a chi ball can be used in any situation, at any time. It is essentially using your mental powers and focused intention to expand and develop the natural chi within and around, and grounding it into an energy ball. This ball of chi can then be used to recharge and re-energize any aspect of yourself. Chi, as you may be aware, is the universal life force which flows through every living thing.

For example, say you are starting to feel fear or nervous tension in a situation due to your empathic sensitivity. You can take a few minutes to close your eyes, become at peace with yourself and 'charge up' an energy ball, and then place it over your heart or stomach (your stomach is your sacral chakra, which is often where tricky, painful, or fear-based emotions arise).

If you ever start to lack insight, you can create a chi ball for your intuition and third eye chakra. If you are starting to question yourself, experience old patterns of low self-esteem or confidence issues through absorbing too much information, the chi ball can be created for your heart chakra. The key is to know that this ball of energy can be created at any time or in any place as the universal life-force energy is always available.

To create your chi ball, visualize a beautiful golden light growing inside your palm chakras. Synchronize your breathing, focus your intention, and really feel this ball of divine energy growing and expanding for your benefit. It is a very effective exercise to incorporate into daily life and can be used to enhance empathy, sight, intuition and any imaginative, creative and intellectual gifts.

Key points:

- Can be used at any time or place
- Only takes a few minutes
- Can be used for any intention or to enhance any quality lacking
- Visualize a glowing ball of beautiful light expanding in between your hands
- Breathe into the chi ball and watch it grow
- Place it over any one of your chakras for the desired healing effect

A short exercise for self-love

This is a very simple yet highly effective exercise for increasing self-love. As explored, self-love is one of the main steps to healing psychology and spiritually, and protecting your boundaries. First, purchase a rose quartz crystal gemstone. Rose quartz specifically relates to the heart and has vibrational qualities of enhancing unconditional love, compassion, kindness, empathy, and forgiveness. Rose quartz is essentially known as the heart chakra stone.

- Cleanse and charge your crystal. Firstly, cleanse your crystal in cold running water and then charge it in direct sunlight. Crystals respond to the natural elements and also pick up and store energy, therefore, it is essential that you cleanse and charge your crystal of any lingering energies.

- Create a sacred space either outside in a favorite nature spot or inside.
- Hold the rose quartz in the palm of your left hand with your right hand hovering over the top. Similar to the visualization expressed earlier, visualize a beautiful, warm and loving glowing light emanating from both the crystal and your right hand. Practice your breathing.
- Make sure your breath is deep, calm, and steady with a slightly euphoric feeling or at least a deep sense of enhanced awareness. Breathe deeply within and into the crystal, still picturing a glowing light growing. Once you feel calm and centered with a steady glow in between your hands and any tingling or energetic sensations, set your intention. Focus your mental power on love, healing, forgiveness, and positive energy filling up the rose quartz. Project these intentions while similarly visualizing and feeling the glowing light.
- Sit with this experience for a while and pour your love and positive energy into the crystal. Once you feel ready, let go of all thoughts and intentions and be still. Keep breathing steady but be still inside your mind, allowing your energy to merge with the crystals. Feel yourself receiving the rose quartz's beautiful healing vibrations of love and forgiveness and feel its subtle pulse interacting with yours.

This short but powerful exercise can be done anywhere and anytime once you have established a connection. You can also purchase rose quartz earrings, pendant or smaller crystal to keep in your pocket or purse and carry around with you. Always remember the intention and inner qualities of rose quartz and allow yourself to receive love on a daily basis.

The science of crystals: *Gemstones have been used for thousands of years due to the knowledge of their healing power. They have metaphysical properties which allow them to be catalysts for healing and wholeness to occur. Nowadays we use quartz crystals to power watches yet ancient cultures were also aware of the inner power of crystals. Essentially the electromagnetic energy field of the crystal or gemstone interacts without the electromagnetic energy field, affecting the mind, emotions, body, and spirit in addition to enhancing the qualities associated with the specific crystal.*

Psychic Awareness exercises

As all of our bodies are connected, increasing your psychic awareness and intuition can lead to enhanced perception, insight, and connection to a higher power. This, in turn, helps you connect to your true empathic nature and embrace the qualities which make you who you are. Your heart (where empathy arises) and higher mind (where your spiritual awareness comes forth) are intrinsically linked.

The crystal exercises can be used to increase your psychic and spiritual awareness, therefore allowing yourself to thrive as an empath. Combine a crystal visualization technique with a hands-on healing technique from this chapter. Once you have become familiar with the essence of these exercises, your intuition will naturally enable you to create your own techniques and exercises for connecting to your spiritual body. There is not greater intuition than the empath intuition!

Chapter 3: The Physical Body

Lifestyle and Energy

One of the main issues many empaths find themselves struggling with until you learn what is occurring and how to overcome it, is the importance of diet and lifestyle on your energy.

Two words which go very well with empath are *clean and pure*. Living a clean and pure lifestyle, to the best of your ability, will allow you to thrive and access your unique gifts in the process.

Growing up you may not have been conscious or innerstood why you felt the way you did. People around you may have eaten certain foods and gained energy whereas you instantly became tired, down, or lethargic. You may have gone through long and frequent periods of depression or low moods without realizing why, and activities which gave others pleasure didn't have the same spark with you.

This is because you operate at a much higher emotional frequency than others. Just as extroverts receive their dopamine rush from external stimuli and interaction, and introverts can create their own dopamine, you receive your joy and delights from emotional stimulation and connection. It is like becoming recharged through the frequency of your own gifts, essentially 'sparking yourself' through your empathic nature.

As we delve into diet and emotions in the next two sections, let's look at other ways you can live a physically pure and clean lifestyle.

How to heal psychologically

As your mind and emotions are intrinsically linked taking steps to heal psychologically will only have a positive effect on your emotions and intuitive and empathic gifts. Understand your inner workings and inner psychology can really help with this. We have already looked at the Self and Carl Jung's shadow archetype, so let's look at some different ways to heal psychologically.

- **Journaling**. Journaling is a really powerful way to heal psychologically. When you journal you are being given complete freedom and space to express yourself and explore your deepest desires and workings. Memories, opinions, perspectives, and observations can all come out through journaling, and there is no one to judge you or tell you something is 'wrong.' This allows you to explore yourself with complete liberation and therefore also aids in self-development, evaluation, and learning. You can explore your deepest shadows, wounds, likes, dislikes, memories, and emotions through writing about them and subsequently grow and heal as an empath. Purchase a special journal and begin to write down your feelings. You could split it into sections like 'Shadow,' 'Past Pains,' 'Past Lessons,' 'Memories,' 'Dreams,' 'Goals, Dreams and Aspirations', and 'Strengths.'

- **Dream**. Looking at your dreams is another profound way to heal and develop your sense of self. It is in dreams where you can learn about your deepest yearnings, desires, and wishes. You can also learn about any hidden repressions or things you may need to work through. Dreams will often tell us direct messages, wisdoms, or insights and offer guidance through the form of symbols, images or dream scenarios. Junglian analysis ties into dream work as do many shamanic ways of dreaming and shamanic approaches to dream interpretation. Transgressing on from journaling, you could always begin your own dream diary and record your dreams for self-analysis, and healing.

- **Psychotherapy**. Psychotherapy takes many forms, therefore, I intuit there will be something encompassed within this spectrum which will be perfect for your personal journey of healing. Some forms of psychotherapy include art therapy, behavioral therapy, cognitive-behavioral therapy, dream analysis, dance therapy, movement and music therapy, neuro-linguistic programming or psychotherapy, psychoanalysis, and Junglian analysis.

How to heal spiritually

The best way to live a pure and clean lifestyle and heal spiritually is to engage in healing, holistic and alternative therapies and shamanic ways of living. Shamanism is arguably the purest lifestyle as shamans, or those with strong shamanic inclinations, live in harmony with the earth and the world's natural ecosystems. They tend not to drink alcohol, consume poisons or chemicals, and tend to leave a very low carbon footprint. They also connect with plants, flowers, herbs, nature, and special rocks and crystals on a daily basis and engage in ceremony and rituals which keep their spirit's pure and energy clean.

There are a variety of holistic and complementary therapies and practices available today to aid in your healing and self-development. Some of these are as follows:

- Self-Hypnosis
- Energy Work
- Shamanism
- Reiki
- Holistic Massage
- Aromatherapy
- Reflexology
- Herbalism
- Cranial-Sacral Therapy
- Kinesiology
- Acupuncture
- Acupressure
- Crystal Therapy
- Indian Head and Face Massage
- Dream Therapy
- Color Therapy
- Chakra and Aura Therapy
- Hypnotherapy
- Meditation and Mindfulness
- Sound Therapy
- Neuro-Linguistic Programming
- Past Life Therapy
- Shiatsu

- Qi Gong, Yoga, and Dance Therapy

How to heal physically

One of the best ways to heal physically external to diet is to engage in movement. This can take many forms such as dance, exercise, yoga or traditional sports, however as being an empath is a holistic experience (due to your spiritual awareness and intuition) let's look at three powerful holistic activities that can help you remove any final blocks or barriers to success. (i.e living your best life!)

- **Chi Kung or Qi Gong.** Chi kung or Qigong is an ancient martial art focusing on movement. The intention of Qi Gong is to restore chi, your inner power, and energy, to help you thrive in all aspects of life. This martial art is a mind-body-spirit system and subsequently takes a mind-body-spirit approach to health. As an empath, this type of exercise is very good for you as it allows you to develop internal strength and work with your inner energy. It is also very gentle and works well with your empathic and often watery nature. Movements are similar to Tai Chi which works with yin and yang and is not very aggressive or competitive. Qigong can allow you to develop stronger boundaries, strengthen your inner system and strengthen the connection between your mind, body, spirit, and emotions. It can also increase self-esteem and confidence, lead to empowerment and also the ability to speak your truth and know yourself. You have a very wise and perceptive mind and outlook, therefore, honing and developing it with a martial art such as Qigong can be very powerfully healing and beneficial to you. Do some research and see if there are any local Chi Kung or Qigong classes in your area, or perhaps book a retreat or see which festivals offer Qigong workshops and sessions. You will be glad you did!

- **Kundalini Yoga.** Yoga has become increasingly more popular and has found its way into western society. One thing which is less popular or well known is Kundalini Yoga. As we explore in detail in the last chapter of this book, your kundalini is your *serpent power*, the spiritual, energetic, and psychic energy which runs through your chakras. It also relates to sexual and creative energy. When there is a block in your kundalini, many aspects of life and self are affected. Kundalini yoga takes a holistic approach to health and allows you to raise and release any trapped energy, tap into your psychic and intuitive gifts, expand creative, and artistic sight and expression, and achieve states of energy, vitality, inner peace, and wholeness. Kundalini yoga can also involve mudras, mantras and the sharing of ancient and insightful wisdom, which for your empath nature is something you may resonate with! Like with Qi Gong, see if there are any

Kundalini Yoga teachers in your area, or think further afield.

- **Shakti Dance**. Shakti dance is a form of dance which allows you to release any blocked energy, remove stagnant emotional energy, energize your third eye - the seat of your intuition, and connect you to your body and spirituality simultaneously. It is based on the principles of yin and yang and takes into consideration the universal life force and interconnected nature of being. It is especially powerful for empaths as it can increase confidence and intuition while being very fun and healing at the same time. Look into Shakti and do some personal research. It is incredibly psychologically healing.

In addition to holistic movements like Qi Gong, Kundalini Yoga, and Shakti Dance all of the healing therapies and avenues in *How to heal spiritually* can be used for a physically pure and clean lifestyle.

The Importance of Diet

As briefly mentioned diet is one of the most profound influencers and shapers of your psychological and spiritual well being. To many non-empathic people, diet just has a physical effect, they can still survive and thrive mentally, psychologically, emotionally, and spiritually. This is because as an empath you are very watery, or yin, due to your emotional nature. Although fire, earth, and air signs can be empathic, extroverted types and non-empaths are predominantly firey or airy (mental). They can, therefore, be seen to be either lacking the water element or possessing significant amounts of air, earth, or fire.

Many people nowadays recognize the elemental nature of we humans and embrace the astrological influences in play which shape and create who we are. Without going into too much detail, we all have a natal chart which is influenced by astrological transits and planets in the sky. At our time of birth, we had a *specific constitution* which went on to shape our personality and inner biology. A significant aspect of this is the nature of the star signs and corresponding elements.

Now although empaths are not necessary 'water signs,' you are very in tune with the water element. This inevitably means that foods which do not harmonize with your inner biology can severely disrupt your constitution and further your mind, mood, and emotions. Just as you are psychic sponge picking up on everyone else's thoughts and feelings, you are also a physical sponge (think of physical/medical empaths) and therefore are deeply influenced by diet.

In *Food and Emotions* we go through specific types of foods you should eat and avoid as an empath so, for now, let's look at some often less explored links and perspectives to do with diet and its subsequent effects.

5 Elements Theory of Chinese Medicine

It is important to look to ancient cultures for their unique wisdom and insights. Many ancient cultures received their knowledge from the earth, from their ancestors and from traditions and wisdom passed down. Ancient Chinese Medicine is one of the main shapers and influencers of many schools of thought and approaches to diet and health seen today. Similarly, many herbalists and ancient herbal folklore and forms of medicine got a lot of things right in terms of the healing properties found in certain herbs and food types. Luckily, I happened to study both herbalism and 5 elements theory, so all of this information is organic (like the pun?!).

5 elements theory of Chinese medicine refers to the awareness that there are 5 elements or unique energy fields existing in our physical universe. These elements are water, wood, fire, earth, and metal. These elements or forces work in a similar way to yin and yang. Just as yin and yang are sought to be balanced and states of harmony and unity achieved, so are the 5 elements. In terms of diet, this means you can look to certain food types and create the *perfect inner balance and constitution*, for your empath nature, based on being aware of the 5 elements.

Let's look at these now.

- Wood makes fire stronger, is helped by water, and can consume earth.
- Fire makes earth, can melt metal, can be made stronger by wood, and stopped by water.
- Earth controls water, contains metal, and can be made by fire.
- Metal cuts wood, improves water, can be contained by earth, and melted by fire.
- Water helps wood grow, can stop fire, can be improved by metal, and stopped by earth.

So how does this relate to diet, you may be wondering?

The 5 elements are not exclusive to the 5 forces. They are also connected to our 5 main organs, 5 colors, and 5 planets. As this topic is about diet, we will just look at the 5 colors and organs. It is also important to know that different organs and bodily systems also have a yin or yang quality and that this is an essential part to Chinese medicine.

Element	Color	Yin	Yang
Wood	Green	Liver	Gallbladder
Fire	Red	Heart	Small Intestines
Earth	Yellow	Spleen	Stomach
Metal	White	Lungs	Large Intestines
Water	Black	Kidneys	Bladder

Obviously, if you are interested in this aspect of diet then this is something you will want to explore in more detail with your own research. The main point to be aware of is that certain foods contain specific qualities and each quality relates to the yin and yang within your own internal systems and a specific color. Practically this means you can look to certain colors to receive inspiration for your food choices.

For example, being aware that green vegetables and leafy greens like cucumber, spinach, kale, and broccoli aid in your *liver,* will allow you to choose foods that can help detoxify and cleanse your liver, while simultaneously increasing your *inner fire* which many empaths lack.

Food and Emotions

In the words of Hippocrates: "Let food be thy medicine and medicine be thy food."

This is a really good saying to remember as an empath.

There are many foods you can eat to help with your empathic nature. Specifically, these include all leafy greens and vegetables, fruits, nuts, and seeds. This is because these food types are high in life force, natural energy, or chi, and help balance your inner systems. The high water content and lightness is soothing and healing on your emotions and also beneficial for your psychic abilities, intuition, and state of mind.

Eating heavy foods or food with little life force can have a very detrimental effect on your chi levels. As emotions are quite a 'heavy' quality (as opposed to air which is light) you need to be particularly careful with the foods you consume.

Here are the top 10 foods you should incorporate into your diet as an empath. They can all assist you in living in a heightened state of awareness and being, maintaining your intuitive and compassionate gifts in the process.

1. **Leafy Greens.** Dark leafy greens raise your vibration. They are high in life force, nutrients, and water content and can help keep you full while *feeling light* simultaneously. They also have a positive effect on your emotions due to being natural and a primary food source. As the mind, body, spirit, and emotions are designed to work in harmony, eating leafy greens will have a profound effect on your emotional and physiological well being as well as your physical and psychological health.

2. **Maca.** Maca is a superfood found in Peru. It provides energy, vitality, and sustenance and is high in life force. It is also known to increase sexual vitality and libido, which for an empath who can often lack fire and be overly emotional is good! One of the main reason maca is beneficial as an empath is due to the stabilizing effect it has on emotions. It can act as a hormonal regulator and balancer and therefore provides both emotional stability and health and energy and vitality simultaneously. Maca is usually consumed in smoothies or when sprinkled on salads.

3. **Walnuts.** There is a reason people call this the brain nut! All nuts are good for keeping your empathic qualities aligned and strong, however, walnuts are one of the best. They have an incredible effect on your brain and therefore psychological well being, and due to the high life force and natural essence of walnuts they can keep you spiritually in tune and perceptive. Walnuts have one of the highest antioxidant compositions of all the nuts therefore including these in your diet will help to reduce and eliminate any stress associated with dealing with toxic characters like energy vamps and narcissists or with sensitivity in general.

4. **Superfood Smoothies.** Superfood smoothies are one of the best ways you can keep your emotional, psychological, and spiritual health strong. The best kinds of milk to use are organic and natural nut milk, like hemp, almond, cashew, hazelnut, or soy milk. These can be mixed with a variety of fruits and superfoods. *Chlorella, spirulina, wheatgrass, lucuma, baobab,* and *moringa* (and *maca*) are all foods which should be included to your smoothie, as they are all very good on your constitution. They are also high in life force, nutrients, and energy and actually aid in your spiritual connection and awareness.

5. **Avocados.** Avocados are loaded with healthy and nutritious nutrients, vitamins and minerals and also contain healthy monounsaturated fats. They have antioxidants which can aid in many bodily functions such as eye and heart health

and have a positive effect on your well being and perception. The reason why avocado is included here is because of its importance in vegetarianism. As you may have noticed, there are no 'meats' included here. This is because of the intrinsic connection eating animals has to the empath nature. Your cells know and are deeply intelligent. Consciousness runs through your veins and your cells just as it streams through your mind. Avocados have such a rich source of protein and good fats that they can be part of a balanced and healthy, compassionate diet.

6. ***Raw Living Food***. Any raw living food such as sprouts and sprouting vegetables are all perfect for your diet. This is because these foods help you develop a connection to spirit and the natural world and keep you functioning at a high emotional frequency. They also enhance your intuition due to the intention of eating foods which are natural and alive.

7. ***Superfruits.*** Like superfoods, superfruits are very effective at helping your thrive emotionally. Superfruits include strawberries, raspberries, blueberries, goji berries, goldenberries, gooseberries, cranberries, and any other berry you come across. They connect you to the natural world and a natural vibration and are high in life force (universal energy). They are pure and can aid in your intuitive and creative abilities due to the natural and water aspect.

8. ***Medicinal Mushrooms***. One of the most powerful foods for you as an empath is to consume medicinal mushrooms. Not only are they high in life force and water content but they are also strongly linked to other types of mushrooms which help expand your consciousness and see life in a unified, spiritual and interconnected way. Medicinal mushrooms include *Reishi, Oyster, Shitake, Maitake, Lions Mane, Cordyceps,* and *Chaga* and they can be drunk as a tea, eaten, or taken as supplements.

9. ***Cacao***. Cacao is also known as raw chocolate and is extremely good for an empath. Cacao is rich in antioxidants, high in nutrients and generally makes you feel good. An interesting thing to know about cacao is that when you drink it, either in a smoothie or as a hot chocolate, the plant leaves it trail on the side of your glass and it *looks like roots*. This shows how high in life force it is and how consuming it can lead to your psychological and spiritual well being. It is a deeply spiritually stimulating food source just like superfoods, superfruits, and medicinal mushrooms.

10. ***Pure and Clean Water***. Although it is not food pure and clean water should arguably be included. This is because one of the fundamental aspects of being an empath is or should be the ability to engage in *regular and mindful fasts*. Consuming too much food or the wrong types of food can leave you depleted,

spiritually closed off and with a clouded intuition, as you are aware. Water is *healing*, it heals and cleanses the system. Just 3-day water fast can cleanse and detox the liver and a 7-day water fast can begin cell regeneration and kick start your immune system. Besides fasting, water is life force in its purest and the water element is what provides you such a fine-tuned intuition and sensitivity to your empathic gifts. If you are ever suffering from heavy emotions or low moods, water can be a game changer. Make sure the water you drink is purified, mountain or spring, and filtered, or even better, reverse osmosis.

Mindful Empathic Eating

In addition to the foods mentioned, there are also techniques you can include to aid in your journey to perfect health and empathic well being. For lack of a better term, we can call this *Mindful Empathic Eating*.

The following three tips are ways in which you can eat mindfully and empathically to aid in your psychological, spiritual, and physical health.

- **Gratitude.** Saying thank you to your food before you eat it and meaning it can really help and have a positive effect on your body, mind, and emotions. This is because your thoughts vibrate out to shape, create, and affect physical reality and matter. Each thought and intention you have ripples out, directly influencing the physical structure of matter. Gratitude is a powerful vibration. Like empathy, it has a magnetic quality to it. Feeling gratitude with depth and sincerity and actively saying thank you, either in your mind or out loud, will have a direct influence on the *vibrational quality and essence* of the food you eat.

- **Sensuality, Stillness, and Silence.** Taking time to eat your food and with an inner stillness can aid in your connection to your inner empathy. Engaging with your senses such as through slowing down and taking in every smell, taste, and texture will help you develop a connection to your food, increasing spiritual awareness simultaneously. This is a form of mindfulness and can lead to much *inner*standing and meditative contemplation.

- **Emotional Connection, not Hunger?** Taking a moment to consider if you are truly hungry or just longing for connection and intimacy can help you thrive as an empath. This is because connection, spirit, and emotion are source energy, a form of food in their own right. Apart from actual nutrients, vitamins, and minerals, food is just energy, a form of sustenance and pleasure. It is easy to turn to food as an empath when you are craving some real connection or deep and authentic conversation or interaction. Being mindful of this fact may be a key to the positive change you are seeking.

Chapter 4: The Mental Body

Intuition and Psychic Ability

One of your most powerful gifts in addition to your compassion, kindness, generosity, and desire to help others in some way, is your natural intuition. Linking in with this are psychic ability and other spiritual gifts.

Without going into too much detail (we could write a whole book on this section alone) your ability to perceive subtle and spiritual energy links greatly to many other aspects of life. Creative, imaginative and artistic abilities can increase as can your mental powers and strength. Telepathy can also be a byproduct of advanced and evolved intuition, emotional connection and emotional intelligence. Telepathy is essentially conversing with another without words on a subtle-energetic level. Dolphins communicate telepathically, as can some other animals. Essentially, it is only we humans who have lost our connection to subtle forms of speech, therefore the empathic ability to feel, sense and communicate on a subtle and spiritual level can arguably be seen as the next stage in human evolution.

Intuitive and psychic ability can all be enhanced with clean and pure living and diet, mindfulness and mind programming exercises, transcendental meditation, advanced sound frequencies and therapy such as binaural beats, and through consciously rewiring the brain through neurological responses.

Mental Boundaries

Just like physical boundaries, *mental boundaries* are extremely important. Have you ever been out and about or in social settings around new people and have begun to feel strange, anxious and on edge? A nervousness took hold, you felt like you couldn't be yourself and that your mind had to protect itself, yet you couldn't explain it?

This is because you are highly sensitive to other people's subtle thoughts and intentions. Even if someone's energy is a bit 'off,' you will pick up on it. You may sense that although this person is friendly, outgoing, and liked in a social situation, there is some facade or falseness going on. Or perhaps they have some very unhealthy, destructive, and harmful beliefs and opinions constructing their energy field.

The best way to deal with this and thrive in the process is to develop strong mental boundaries. You can do this in a number ways such as through brain training and strengthening exercises, techniques, and activities to enhance your intuition and psychic ability or spiritual perception, and through working with special gemstones and divinatory objects. Divination is essentially connecting to some natural object or entity which increases your connection to the divine. There is nothing supernatural about it, but it is *super*natural (positive associations only).

The first way to help protect your mind and strengthen your mental boundaries is by working with special gemstones or crystals. Science has shown that crystals can be used to have a number of positive effects and quartz crystals specifically have been used to power watches due to the electromagnetic effect and connection to the natural world. Ancient Egyptians and many other ancient cultures were aware of the power of rare gemstones in their healing abilities and many people today are becoming increasingly more knowledgeable and increasingly less ignorant as to their healing powers. (Refer back to *How to Protect your Energy: Techniques and Exercises*)

The other main method to help with mental boundaries as an empath is to engage in daily *meditation and mindfulness* exercises. Meditation and mindfulness are two of the most profound ways to enhance your sense of self, remain confident and aligned/centered, and live your life free from external disruption or harm.

As an empath who is naturally in tune with some spiritual, subtle, or subconscious aspect of reality, you may not require the science behind meditation and mindfulness. This is because you learn from *experience*, you actually feel the beauty, bliss, and wonder from connecting to your inner being and mental powers from meditation. For the purpose of balance, however, let's explore some of the scientific studies showing the power of meditation and mindfulness. These can be explored to help innerstand some of the exercises in chapter 2.

Meditation

- A study by *Psychosomatic Medicine Journal of Biobehavioral Medicine* found that mindfulness meditation positively affects brain and immune functioning, specifically increasing positive emotions. [2]

---

[2] https://journals.lww.com/psychosomaticmedicine/Abstract/2003/07000/Alterations_in_Brain_and_Immune_Function_Produced.14.aspx

- Research from the *American Psychological Association* discovered that meditation improves positive emotions and enhances loving-kindness.[3]

- Another study shared in the American Psychological Association shows how meditation increases social connection and emotional intelligence. [4]

Mindfulness

- Research published in *Cognitive Therapy and Research* (Volume 28 Issue 4) shows how mindful meditation helps to overcome depression. [5]

- A mindfulness experiment conducted by *Stanford University* discovered that mindfulness for compassion cultivation works. [6]

In truth, there are too many studies to mention however they all fundamentally show the power and effects of mindfulness and meditation on enhancing the self and improving life in some way. Of course, as an empath, you probably already knew all of this! This is the beauty of your gift.

Social Situations and Society

In this section, we will be looking at what it means to be an *introverted empath* and *an extroverted empath*, and how they overlap. This is because all of the information in this book relates directly to social situations and society, therefore, the best way to release any last blocks or barriers to self- mastery (thriving) is to look to your 'sister superpower' for wisdom and integration. This sister superpower is the power of the introvert/extrovert dynamic.

An introverted empath embodies the qualities of an introvert. These qualities are an aversion to big groups or loud social gatherings, a preference of one-to-one or small group interactions, and inner contentment with solitude and solo activities. There is a

---

[3] https://psycnet.apa.org/record/2008-14857-004

[4] https://psycnet.apa.org/record/2008-13989-015

[5] https://link.springer.com/article/10.1023/B:COTR.0000045557.15923.96

[6] http://ccare.stanford.edu/article/enhancing-compassion-a-randomized-controlled-trial-of-a-compassion-cultivation-training/

strong introspective quality to introverts and many introverted personalities thrive in creative, artistic or imaginative realms of thought and being. Extroverts, on the other hand, thrive in social situations and receive their stimulation as such. They are confident, highly expressive and love small- talk, or just any talk really. They are not defined by lacking depth and authenticity, however, they are defined as being happy with meaningless talk and often excessive speaking. Extroverts may be dramatic or the life and soul of a party or social situation.

As an empath, it may be clear by now that one of the best ways to heal and overcome your sensitivities and often overly- emotional nature is to embody some of the characteristics of an extrovert. Now, this does not mean you have to compromise or sacrifice your true nature, it simply means that it may be worth your while to *balance and adapt,* so you are better able to exist in social situations. This is especially true if you find yourself taking on the more negative characteristics of an introvert, such as anxiety, nervous tension, shyness, or self-esteem and confidence issues.

Taking steps to be less introverted or introspective can help you maintain mental clarity and your own inner alignment. This does not mean you have to start shouting, acting like your extrovert non-empathic friends or stop being insightful and intuitive, but it is implying that making a conscious effort to be more social and outwardly expressive can help you overcome some of the uncertainties, confusions, and anxiousness you may feel with picking up on everyone's things. Remember - thoughts, emotions, impressions underlying energy currents, and feelings all become available to you, therefore in a social situation around lots of people, and particularly with many noises and excess sensory information, being less of an introverted empath can be a form of protection in itself.

Another important element to link here is the importance of grounding and centering your energy. The *Tree Meditation* Grounding exercise in Chapter 2 can really help with this. Grounding and centering yourself will allow you to not only cope, but thrive, in social gatherings and situations, keeping your emotional intelligence clear and your mind on point.

The best way to see yourself is like a compass on a ship or small boat. If the magnetic pull is dodgy and the boat keeps spinning round in different directions, there will be no direction. The compass will tell you that you are going one way and then another, and then another, to the point that the compass loses focus and gets pulled around by the currents. You are like the compass. So instead of picking up on everyone else's energy and currents stay centered to your own story, reality, vibe, and truth, and project it out so you can meet people on the level you wish to meet them. Even if it so happens that you play silent observer, quiet introspective one or only connect with one or two people, at least you will be maintaining inner clarity and confidence, and not being dragged around by the tides. All feelings of nervousness, tension, or discomfort can be released in this way.

So to really shine and be in your element in society and social gatherings, engage in meditation, mindfulness and aura strengthening and protecting exercises on a daily basis. Also, remember to take the time you need to recharge in nature or in solitude and pay respect to your inner needs and intuition. Your mental clarity comes with your emotional stability and intelligence.

Chapter 5: The Emotional Body

The Importance of Inner Balance

I am sure you are already aware of this due to your natural intuition and feel what is best for your highest joy... but let's express it again. *Inner balance* is your new power term!

Empathy is defined by emotion, being emotional, feeling an emotional connection to others, and using your emotional sensitivity and wisdom to assist others in some way, whether it being in daily life or channeled into a profession. Your ability to operate at a higher vibrational frequency emotionally than others is your greatest strength, yet also your potential greatest downfall. Learning how to develop inner balance and keep yourself in a healthy emotional state could possibly be one of the most significant factors in your journey to healing and wholeness.

The body is designed to maintain and develop equilibrium. As you are aware, the human system is complex and consists of many different bodies or layers. As an empath, you operate in your emotional body consistently and at all times, even when you are connected to your higher mind, intellect, spiritual self, or psychic physical being. This means that you can often get drained, feel and take on other people's low moods or pains (on an inner, emotional level), and need to take frequent periods to recharge and reconnect to your own source of inner power. Nature is one of the most profound ways to do this!

How to Deal with Emotional Overload

Try this aura strengthening and protecting exercise for dealing with emotional overload and putting up better boundaries.

- Begin by getting into a meditative position. This can be inside in a comfortable spot or outside in your favorite nature spot. Make sure you are undisturbed. If you have music handy this technique works particularly well with certain musical healing tones. These include nature sounds such as gentle running water or rain, bird song, or whale or dolphin song; Tibetan singing bowls, chimes, or bells, or gentle and rhythmic shamanic drumming. If you are familiar with binaural beats you can also use binaural beats as a background sound therapy.

- Close your eyes and take your awareness inside. Start by taking some deep breaths and focusing on your breathing, drawing your awareness inside. See a shining white light around your sacral chakra, your emotional center, and watch it grow gently as you breathe. This technique is visualization and it is very powerful working on your subtle energy bodies, aura and spiritual body.

- After you feel connected to the visualization and feel relaxed and calm within, in a meditative state, bring your hands up to in front of your heart. Keep your palms facing each other in a ball like position and begin to create a chi ball. Watch this ball of pure white light energy grow and expand, and take your time with the process.

- Continue to focus on your breath and see the white light glowing around your sacral, while simultaneously expanding the energy inside your ball of chi. Set the intention for healing and to release any emotional wounds, traumas or issues holding you down. Project this intention into your ball of chi now and do so in any way which intuitively feels right for you. For example, you may visualize the words directly inside the chi ball and watch them expand and amplify, or you may use your powers of projection on a more subtle layer.

- Once you feel that your white light ball of energy is fully energized and you are in an energetic space to receive the full effects, bring it down in front of your sacral. At this point, you should be in a mildly euphoric state and even feel transcendental. Now you are ready to receive this healing energy.

- The rest will intuitively flow. Once you pour the ball of energy into your sacral emotional center allow yourself to sit with the feeling. Become aware of what is occurring on an energetic and deeper level, how the white light is removing any blocks or negative energy from your energy field and how it is simultaneously strengthening your emotional center and inner boundaries. You can shift your awareness to any aspect of consciousness which feels right for you, however, do not force anything, simply allow and be open to receive.

- Finish the visualization meditation with coming back into your center and setting a blessing or intention. You are aware at this stage that your cells are conscious, intelligent and aware so converse with them. Feel your emotional center, your chakras, and your subtle energy bodies and feel your cells and inner being. Speak positive, loving and healing intentions and thoughts to yourself and simply allow yourself to receive and heal.

This meditation is often called a white light meditation, visualization meditation, core programming meditation or an aura healing and protection (exercise). They key is to *feel* and connect to your empathic nature to be open to receive. It is very powerful.

Famous (Emotional) Empaths

It is important when exploring our own nature to look to some of the world's famous empaths who have shaped history. With anything in life, without personal connection and first-hand experience, there can be room for 'intuitive guessing' and insightful perception - i.e. there are no physical records stating these people were empaths. However, they are people who significantly displayed empathic qualities through their work, teachings or service and therefore can be seen to be highly empathic.

Let's have a look at some of these now. See if you can see any similarities in yourself.

Mahatma Gandhi

Mahatma Gandhi is probably the first person you think of when you think 'famous or well-known empath.' Gandhi is one of the most well-known campaigners for Indian Independence and inspired thousands if not millions of people through his deep emotive abilities.

Mahatma Gandhi was born and raised in a Hindu merchant caste and came from a well off and fortune family. He swapped this life for dhoti (an Indian loincloth) and ashram life and stepped into the shoes of the peasants and farmers. He was deeply disturbed and moved by the violence and deep hatred between Muslims and Hindus and, although he was Hindu himself, became an activist for religious peace and harmony. One of his most famous statements, which arguably shows him as an empath, and a powerful one, was saying to fellow Hindus: "I am a Muslim! And a Hindu, and a Christian and a Jew. So are all of you."

Empath Characteristics:

- He had no desire for riches and material comforts. He happily gave these up for simple ashram life.

- He was a political and religious activist. Gandhi spent his life working towards peace, harmony, and cooperation and eventually died for his beliefs and convictions.

- Had the ability to connect to others on a deep level and showed deep displays of compassion and higher emotional functioning.

Claiborne Paul Ellis

Claiborne Paul Ellis was the leader of the Ku Klux Klan after following his father's footsteps, who eventually realized the error of his ways and the life he had born into. He became great friends with a black activist called Ann Atwater and subsequently became one of the most well known civil rights campaigners and a labor organizer for a predominantly black union. His transition and awakening portrays quite clearly the power of empathy and learning through a connection on a deep level.

Empath Characteristics:

- Despite being raised with some strong and deeply ingrained mindsets and beliefs, Paul Ellis evolved and changed his ways to a reality rooted in connection, empathy, and equality.

- He overcame the wounds and traumas of his past and rose to new heights rooted in community, compassion and universal truth.

- Bravery. He was willing to renounce his ways with potential expense to his family ties for what he believed was right.

Hilary Swank

Hilary Swank is possibly another of the world's most famous empaths due to her role in *Boys Don't Cry,* in which she won an Oscar for her deeply empathic and empowering performance. She played the role of Brandon Teena, a real-life transgender man who was raped and murdered after being found out he had female genitalia. After Hilary Swank took on and played this role she began a path of becoming a campaigner and spokesperson of gay, lesbian, and transgender rights and issues, in addition to raising global awareness.

Empath Characteristics:

- She had a deeply developed connection to her role and the empathy which accompanied.
- She was inspired by the struggles, pain, and suffering of others. Hilary Swank chose a path which helped others as a result.
- The ability to merge with and connect with a role which wasn't her personality. This is a deeply empathic gift to possess!

In addition to these three world-class empaths, many empaths take a role in the musical, acting, performing and creative and artistic fields due to your ability to merge with other characters, archetypes, images or ideas.

Chapter 6: The Spiritual Body

Cleansing, Clearing, and Alignment

The spiritual body is a complex yet simple thing. Spirit is essentially everything, everything consists of a spiritual-energetic essence. Just like we have an aura or electromagnetic field we also have a spiritual element. Spirit and the spiritual body, however, are not synonymous.

It is significant when looking into the spiritual body to see how to survive and thrive as an intuitive empath that you first define and innerstand the different parts to it. The Spiritual body consists of the astral body or the aura, the etheric body and the soul. Each one has its own links and associations, and each one simultaneously links to the other bodies- the mental body, the emotional body, and the physical body. In this section, we will just explore the astral, etheric and soul bodies.

The Astral Body

The astral body is an energetic blueprint of the physical body. It corresponds to the aura, the invisible but very real energy field that encompasses and protects us from external harm and negative influence (or is supposed to). Just as all natural phenomena have an electromagnetic energy field, so do us. As briefly explored earlier, the electromagnetic energy field and aura are one and the same; both are terms to describe the same thing but from different schools of thought. In Buddhist, Taoist, and spiritual philosophies, the aura is, in essence, the same as what science defines as an electromagnetic energy field. Eastern religions and ancient belief systems, however, go a step further and recognize the real-life implications and applications.

We can not only use our auras to protect but to also influence and shape physical reality as we know it. The astral body, where the aura is found, is connected to the mental, emotional, physical, and spiritual planes of existence. Any thought, belief, impression, intention, direction of awareness, or 'inner action' ripples out into one's astral body. Essentially, the mind continuously influences this unseen and invisible energetic barrier and protects one from harm and negative influence. This, in turn, has a powerful effect on every experience and interaction.

You can embody a certain story, archetype, mood, chakra, character, or persona and people will naturally respond to it. For example, people will just know when you want to be left alone and have your own space as you will radiate this through your thoughts. When you are excited and joyous, your feeling radiates outward and others respond accordingly. This is because the aura is powerful and extends far beyond the realm of the five physical senses. In terms of being an empath, you can not only protect yourself, but also use the astral body to empower, help, support, and connect to the intuitive and spiritual gifts you possess.

It is in the astral body where you pick up and receive other people's emotions, feelings, and thoughts. This can lead to many of the struggles of being an empath as explored earlier however can simultaneously act as a bridge to your unique spiritual and psychic or perceptive gifts. Taking time to connect to your astral body, through aura strengthening and protecting exercises and making conscious intentions to do so, can lead to some profound effects and positive changes in your life!

The Etheric Body

The etheric body is often confused with astral body as they are very similar and share similar functions, however, they are not identical. The astral body and your aura relate to the electromagnetic field surrounding you and how you pick up on others' emotions, whereas the etheric body is an energetic replica of your physical body. It is the layer of self just beyond the physical which is responsible for the manifestation of all illness, disease and ill-thought and belief on *a soul level*.

Many energy workers and healers work on the ether, or on the etheric body, as they recognize that healing disease and energy blockages or distortions in this space reflects directly into the physical. As an empath, this means that through engaging in exercises which work on your etheric body you can overcome any blockages or ailments on a physical level. As you are aware, beliefs, thoughts and mental constructs are all intrinsically connected to the physical world, therefore being knowledgeable of this and integrating it as a truth into daily life can help you survive and thrive in your empathic gifts.

The Soul

The soul shapes all aspects of life. It is the part of self which exist beyond space and time, and beyond the three-dimensional and often limiting reality we reside in. All of our soul's experiences, learnings, integrations, and discoveries are encompassed in the soul, which stems beyond this one lifetime. Regardless of whether one believes in reincarnation in itself, the soul is very real as there is an eternal, energetic element to ourselves which is not bound to the one physical body we currently reside in.

All of our thoughts, beliefs, and subconscious programming and life choices, therefore, are influenced by our soul. We also have the power to recreate our lives and future choices based on the choices we make today, in each moment of now. Being conscious and aware of our thoughts, feelings, and emotions therefore control and hold real power over the person we are becoming, the careers and paths we choose, and the potential lives we will inhabit. Life itself is an evolutionary journey and on some deeper level, you have chosen to be an empath in this life.

Now, this has great implications. If you choose to be an empath then you essentially have given yourself the foundation, struggles, and lessons desired to grow and evolve. You wanted the empath experience, the suffering, the hardships and the painful lessons to develop your gifts and become the beautiful, unique and empathic being you were destined to be.

All of life is temporary and things are in constant motion. Nothing ever stays the same, so ultimately the struggles and trials of an empath are the tests you yourself provided, on a soul level, to take you to the next level. Empaths can arguably be seen as the next stage in the evolutionary journey!

The Importance of Discernment

One thing that you will find or may have already found on your empath journey is the importance of discernment. You are brilliant. You are a beautiful, wise, and sincere soul, yet so many people take advantage of your kindness and willingness to give. Until you learn how to protect your energy and be centered and sovereign inside, you literally project an aura that screams "come and unload all your sh*t on me!" It is completely unconscious but it is very real.

As explored earlier your aura is the energetic bubble around you responsible for your thoughts, beliefs, impressions, and emotions. It is perpetually transmitting, receiving and interacting with energy, both the energy in your immediate surroundings and all energy connected in a quantum holographic field. As the way you think and perceive influences your aura, you can often leave yourself open to other people's 'stuff.' This is because you see the world in a compassionate, caring, and empathic way and unconsciously take on the role of the healer, even if just inside.

So people gravitate towards this and feel that they can unload and even sometimes project their own problems, wounds, and pains onto you. Most of the time it is not vindictive, as we will explore in a moment, and people really do just magnetize to your compassion and sight, however, some people see this as a chance to project their own shadow and darkness and dump it on you.

To discern is to judge, but in a sensitive, healthy, and insightful way. In this sense it can be seen that you often *lack judgment* and thus unconsciously open yourself up to unwanted energies, realities, and interactions.

Let's look at some real-life situations you may often find yourself residing in.

A Stranger's Shoulder to Cry On

Strangers will often come up to you when sat alone on a park bench or when strolling through your favorite nature spot. This is because they naturally gravitate to you and your *inner magnetism*. You have a magnetic pull which people sense and even the non-psychic ones! Others sense your compassionate nature and feel drawn to you.

This may manifest as directly seeking your guidance and wisdom or by simply being next to you. You have a powerful presence in which people respond positively to. Of course, this is a beautiful gift and I would never suggest otherwise. Many truly appreciate your empathy and unconditional love and compassion you exhibit. However, if you are not careful, this can leave you drained and depleted and furthermore prevent you from living your best life for you. If you are always giving, sharing your wisdom and holding space for others how can you possibly be there for yourself? Learning discernment in situations like these is one of the best things to do to protect and conserve your energy and the best way to thrive and survive as an empath.

One of the most effective ways to do so is through boundary and aura strengthening exercises. Being open to helping stranger's in need can allow you to shine your beautiful qualities and strengthen your own confidence and self-esteem in the process. It can also energize and amplify the gifts you are displaying, such as your unique sight, wisdom, and intuition. However, this needs to be balanced with learning when to put up a boundary and enjoy your own company or activity you are doing. You may have gone for a walk in nature or to sit on a bench admiring the birds and trees because you need to recharge yourself or to contemplate and introspect on something important in your life. This is where balance and discernment come in, and why they are essential to develop and integrate.

An Emotional Dump Ground

Unfortunately, you can often become everyone's emotional dump ground! Again, this is due to your compassionate and caring nature, however, this does not serve yourself in any way shape or form. Your beautiful qualities and intuitive sight should be honored, respected and appreciated; not abused, taken advantage of and disrespected. Friends and family who may have once appreciated your empathic nature may become insensitive and selfish in their ways and their connection with you, and because you are such a natural helper and healer at heart you simply overlook it or tell yourself the story that they are sincere and pure in their intentions.

Learning discernment can help you realize when someone you love and care for really is starting to abuse your kindness and generosity. We all have a dark side and no one is perfect. Accepting this and recognizing that if a close friend temporarily does this it does not define them, can help you heal the relationships with yourself and thus heal your relationship with them. It is so true that our relationship with ourselves sets the stage for our relationship with others. Treating yourself with love and kindness will allow your empathic gifts and qualities to shine when they are truly needed.

A Narcissist, Energy Vampire or Toxic Person Magnet

Finally, your lack of discernment can leave you as a magnet for toxic personalities. Narcissists become attracted to your open aura, inner beauty and kindness and seek to unload their shadow, and energy vampires do the same but seek to take all you have. Other toxic personalities even go so far as to abuse and intentionally cause you real pain and suffering. You are like a magnet for these types of personalities and often have 'rose-tinted glasses' for vision until you reach a certain maturity and innerstanding.

We explore this in detail in the next chapter.

Chapter 7: Innerstanding the Dynamics between an Empath and Narcissists and Energy Vampires

Narcissists and Energy Vampires: Who are they?

As you now have a firm innerstanding of what it means to be an empath, and your various 'bodies,' strengths and talents, and potential pitfalls, in this section we will take an in-depth look at the empath-narcissist relationship and other toxic personalities such as energy vampires. An integral part of the empath journey is the attracting and defending of narcissists and other toxic peoples. Narcissists are drawn to you as you are literally polar opposites. They seek your purity, inner beauty, and compassionate heart, and feed off you in some way. Let's look at this further.

Narcissists

Unlike you who is inherently selfless, giving, kind, and empathic, narcissists are inherently selfish. They are defined by what they can take and lack compassion, and sometimes to extremes. Narcissists thrive off drama and find solace in your despair. It feeds them and regardless of how much time, love, energy, or resources you have shared they often don't care about your suffering or the pain they may have caused. These characters are highly toxic and often magnetize to your personality, as we will explore in *The Empath-Narcissist Relationship*.

Energy Vampires

Energy vampires are a drain on your energy. They may drain you emotionally, mentally, physically or spiritually, or may suck you dry of your resources, love, compassion, and money. However it manifests, the result of being in a relationship of friendship with an energy vampire will leave you depleted and lacking in strength. These characters can also really affect your confidence and self-esteem as they make you question yourself due to your lack of energy. They become so attracted to your light that they leave you suffering silently in darkness!

The Empath-Narcissist Relationship

The empath-narcissist relationship is possibly one of the most profound struggles to your journey as an empath and something you will undoubtedly face. When you find yourself in a relationship with a narcissist (which you won't realize at first but only once you are in deep), you can either entertain them, stay put and allow the vicious cycles of suffering, trauma, and pain; or you can leave and go your own way. You will *always* choose the route to be free of a narcissist as no empath can stay in that energetic space for too long without causing serious harm and ill-health to self, however, the time period in which to do so may vary.

Let's look at the key components of an empath-narcissist relationship:

- You are initially attracted to their charm and apparent wisdom. A Narcissist has a charming and kind persona as, to begin within, they mirror what they know you possess.

- They want to appear in a positive light. A narcissist loves appearing in a positive and beautiful light. This is mainly so when they are 'found out' later they have a cover story or projected image which others may believe.

- The relationship is defined by imbalance, selfishness, and manipulation. Narcissists are selfish and are primarily about what they can take. Similar to an energy vampire they may drain you of your love, time, affection, resource, kindness, heart, or spirit, and always make you feel bad or guilty about it through manipulation. They are highly manipulative and can leave you feeling emotionally destroyed.

- Pain, suffering, and trauma is frequent in the empath-narcissist relationship. This is always on your part. The narcissist doesn't care and can shock you at their lack of compassion. They thrive in your suffering and lack the empathy that you possess.

- The unconditional love and depth you reflect are met back with an illusion. You develop a deep bond with your narcissistic partner as you truly believe they are mirroring the qualities you hold true and dear, however it is ultimately a deception and over time they reveal their true colors. At this point it is (nearly) impossible to break free and leave the bond.

- The narcissist makes you question yourself, your intuition, your knowledge and, over time, your own heart and values.

- Due to your love and need for deep emotional connection, it can be hard to innerstand that the narcissist's shadow, wounds, and ways are not your own. Your belief and truth that we are all a reflection of one another, and that you want to be compassionate, loving, and accepting, can leave you in a deep state of confusion and ultimately victimhood. Sacrifice, inner suffering, and the victim-martyr-savior complex can take over any real and sincere feelings you once had in your attempt to please and keep the connection intact.

As you can see this is not a healthy or happy connection. Yet when you are in that space, and especially due to their initial charm, it can be very hard to get out of. Luckily the empath personality is strong and with such positive self-love and self-respect that you will never choose to stay in this toxic relationship for too long a period of time.

You may be drawn into the drama and toxicity for a short time frame, but you always come out of it much wiser, stronger and with your empathic qualities shining more brightly than ever. There is only light at the end of this dark tunnel!

Taking Back Your Power!

This brings us to taking back your power. Quite simply, and something you already know deep within, this all comes up to boundaries, grounding, and strengthening your aura and your centeredness within. You are a very wise, humble, and powerful being, dear empath, yet allowing toxic characters to treat you the way do is setting a bad example not only to yourself but to how you allow other potential characters to treat you. Self-love is one of the most powerful ways to heal from these sorts of relationships, and fortunately, there are many methods to self-love.

In addition to the *Self-love exercise* and *Rose Quartz healing* (which are very significant here) begin to incorporate these methods into your life. You will notice a profound change in your energy, inner confidence, and self-esteem and your ability to deal with narcissistic and unsavory characters in the future. Wearing an *amethyst pendant* for protection and engaging in *brain strengthening mindfulness and mind programming exercises* too can really help.

Techniques for Self-love:

- **Self-care.** One of the greatest ways to practice self-love is to engage in daily or frequent self-care. This can include self-massage, treating yourself with pampering and loving your body with healthy and nutritious foods such as superfood smoothies and raw cacao hot chocolates. Take the time for yourself and you will see how this powerfully affects your inner confidence and natural boundaries.

- ***Receive Healing***. Receiving healing either through therapy, energy healing, or peer support or counseling can really help. There are many avenues of healing and some may not feel right for you. For example, you may resonate more with hands-on therapies such as Indian head massage, holistic massage, or crystal therapy, or you may feel more inclued to speaking with an experienced dream therapist, hypnotherapist, or past-life regression therapist. Meditating and connecting to your inner nature and soul can offer you the guidance for what you may be needing.

- ***Following your Passions***. The best way to regain your personal power and connect to your true nature is to do what you love. Taking time to engage in your favorite hobby, spending time with close friends or following your own personal dreams, passions and aspirations will naturally distance yourself from any toxic or destructive connection you may find yourself entangled in. It begins with small steps but over time your internal energy field will lose its magnetic pull towards those who pull you out of your alignment and integrity.

- ***Meditate on Compassion***. Meditating on compassion and self-love can help enhance the qualities within. This is because when you meditate you energize that which you give your attention to. You also release all that no longer serves your highest joy or self in the process. Mindful meditation can also be very effective at changing your thought patterns and neurological responses to certain situations and energy plays or interactions, as mindfulness is a form of mental reprogramming in itself.

Chapter 8: How to Use Your Gifts to Help Others and the World

The Beautiful Gift of Empathy

Empathy is a beautiful gift. The world arguably needs more of you due to your inner purity, natural beauty, and unique way of perceiving and experiencing the world. Your compassion, kindness, and depth of spirit know no bounds, and people see this. Hopefully, by now, you have learned that narcissists, energy vampires, and other toxic personalities have no role to play in your life. You have also learned how to strengthen your boundaries within and protect yourself, therefore your natural gifts and positive qualities can thrive.

You are the dreamers, healers, helpers, and caring people of our world, with unlimited compassion and universal love. You are also one of the most intuitive, imaginative, and creatively gifted types of people in existence. Yet with great power comes great responsibility, even if just for yourself.

In the next section, we look at *The Chakra System* and how you can heal yourself for good and on all levels. Before we do this, let's briefly explore the types of careers that are best suited to yourself and all empaths around today. If you are yet to find your personal path then this list may help you or 'spark' something within which you were not previously aware of, or if you were aware of it but needed that final confirmation. Remember; you are already empowered as you are already powerful! You just need to *let go* and release all of the stuff that is not yours and was never yours to begin with.

Best Careers for an Empath

- Psychologist
- Dream Therapist or Interpreter
- Musician
- Artist

- Writer
- Philosopher
- Nurse
- Physician
- Holistic or Complementary Therapist
- Massage Therapist
- Social or Support Worker
- Veterinarian
- Animal Welfare or Rescue
- Environmentalist
- Landscape Gardener
- Campaigner
- Speaker
- Teacher
- Charity Worker or Leader
- Non-Profit Organization Leader or Worker
- Counselor
- Life Coach
- Healer
- Shaman
- Hospice Worker
- Spiritual Teacher, Speaker, or Healer
- Tarot Reader or Psychic

As you can see, this list is rather eclectic! All these professions, however, tap into some aspect of your personality and inherent nature, meaning that you would thrive in any of these careers or paths.

The Chakra System: Creating Harmony and Wholeness Within

One of the most important teachings it is important to be aware of when embarking on a journey of healing and wholeness is to become in tune with your chakras.

All illness, disease and innate psychological conditions can be seen to have their origins in something internal. There is not only the physical reality and we are complex beings. We are shaped by our experiences, observations, hardships, struggles, interactions, sensory stimuli, and inner biological factors. Every sound heard, sight witnessed, and touch experienced contributes to the person we know as the self. All of our beliefs, conditioned thought patterns, and inner emotional responses are therefore influenced by the external world.

Many people around the world believe and recognize that there is an invisible element to life. Just as we dream at night and our mind drifts into another reality, we are governed by our subconscious and the collective consciousness. The subconscious is the 'behind the scenes' element to life which is responsible for our hidden motives, impressions, beliefs, feelings and subtle thoughts. The collective consciousness is the shared aspect to self, the collective mind, which is an accumulation of every human's individual beliefs, thoughts, intentions, and impressions. Both have a profound effect on daily life and the ego.

Now, when we refer to the ego it is not inherently 'bad.' Of course, it is natural to assume that ego is predominantly negative as many of the harmful, wrong and inhumane acts we see nowadays are committed by those who are 'in their ego.' The same can be said for excessive greed, spite, hatred, selfishness and all other lower human characteristics. However, essentially the ego is a fundamental part of the self and we wouldn't exist without it. It is the individual part of our whole which makes us unique.

It is, however, one part of the self, and this is a key point to remember. The whole human is a complex and interacting being of mind, emotions, feelings, and spirit. There are many layers and reality is not just defined by the often limited, purely physical five senses way of perceiving. So steering back towards those invisible and unseen elements of self, *the chakra system* is a very beneficial belief system and area of thought to look into when learning about the empath personality and how to thrive in all aspects of life, specifically psychologically and spiritually.

Many believe, including but not limited to those who practice a spiritual path, ancient cultures, and Taoists, that the physical body is governed by chakras or energy portals.

These are the unseen yet highly real energetic aspects to the whole self and can be learned about and connected with to heal many aspects of daily life. Just as every living thing on earth possesses an electromagnetic energy field, so do we. This electromagnetic energy field is also known as our aura and relates to the astral body. The astral body is the energetic replica of our physical body and many ancient cultures and people were aware that by healing the astral body and aura mental, emotional, physical and spiritual ailments could too be healed. In other words, any illness or disease which manifests in the physical or physiological self can be seen to have its origins in the astral body.

Empathy and all its various struggles are a manifestation of the unseen elements to life, the situations, experiences, observations and interactions which have shaped your upbringing. It is important therefore to look at the whole self, including those invisible and energetic aspects to the empath personality to help heal it and bring wholeness and inner harmony.

Let's now look at the chakra system in detail and expand our awareness of how the beautiful gift of empathy can be harnessed and self- mastered through deeper inner work.

The Root or Base Chakra

This is your foundation. It relates to your sense of security, connection to the earth and your own body, and physical vitality. The associated colors are red (primary) and brown. The element is earth.

This chakra is very important as it is from this center, your root, which sexuality and kundalini energy is created and rises. Your kundalini is your serpent power, the snake-like coil of energy which flows from your base up your spine to your head or your crown chakra. Physically, it is responsible for your vitality, physical health and energy levels, and your sexual energy. It also corresponds to your physical chi and life-force energy and on the mental and emotional planes of existence links to your mental power, emotional wisdom and maturity, and psychic and intuitive abilities.

If the root chakra is blocked, then all the other chakras will be blocked, and sexual or kundalini energy will not be able to flow freely. As an empath, you can often be in your head and out of your body. In this sense, problems which arise for empaths are frequently regarding their disconnection from the physical body. This manifests of course as problems in intimate relationships and also the sacral chakra, which is responsible for emotions. We explore this next.

The Sacral Chakra

This is also known as your sex center in that it is the center of your emotions, creativity, and sexuality. The related color is orange and the element is water. This, therefore, is where empaths have most problems. As the corresponding element is water and the sacral chakra is your emotional and sexual center, many repressed emotions, traumas, and wounds become stored over time. As you will see in the next chakra, this strongly affects the solar plexus - your sense of vitality, self-empowerment, and confidence.

All chakras are linked and connected, therefore any problems in one's energy center affects the others, more so the ones next to it. The sacral chakra can be meditated on and there are exercises for self-healing which can be done to help bring ease and healthy chi to this area. As an empath, you may have problems in this chakra which can manifest as stomach aches and pains or digestive disorders until you heal yourself and learn how to be centered and strong in your boundaries.

The Solar Plexus Chakra

The solar plexus chakra, as briefly outlined, is your sense of self-empowerment, vitality, and confidence. It is also your expression, will, and ego and relates to ambition.

The color for this chakra is yellow and the element fire. It also can be seen as 'sunny' as it links to your will, ego, vitality, and empowerment. Empaths usually suffer from confidence and self-esteem issues; therefore, this is where physical manifestations may show. All the chakras affect the physical, mental, emotional and spiritual bodies in some way, so any disruption or energy block will intrinsically affect all other areas of the self.

Regarding confidence and self-esteem specifically, if you are in a particularly low mood and are lacking in the beautiful confidence you possess, the effect this has on your solar plexus actively affects your sacral and your heart chakra. If you are suffering from confidence issues, then you are not fully connected to your heart space and the compassion, genuine kindness, and empathic qualities you embody. Simultaneously, you are not in harmony with your own emotions and you will experience blockages, distortions, and nervous tension there.

As you are very sensitive and affected by other's moods, intentions, energies, and emotions, in sexual relationships any slight disruption or issue has a very profound effect on the rest of the chakras. Empaths can often take on every single judgment, projection, thought, emotion and trauma of their partner and store it (unconsciously) in their sacral chakras. This, of course, has an intrinsic effect on the solar plexus and your confidence and self-worth.

It is important that as an empath, you to learn how to protect yourself, stay aligned to your own inner truth and sense of worth, and stay committed to your dreams and personal wills. The exercises throughout this book can help you do this!

Heart Chakra

This is your heart center and relates to empathy, kindness, compassion, generosity, love, unconditional universal love, and also your connection to nature and the natural world. Empaths usually have a very strong heart chakra, which is a blessing as it is the center, therefore affecting all other chakras!

In intimate relationships, however, it can be hard to find a partner 'on your wave.' Due to the initial charm of narcissistic people, you will often attract those who simply aren't on your wave and don't share in your values. When older, however, it will become easier to stay centered and make the right decisions with such a powerful heart chakra. You will naturally draw partners to you who share your empathic qualities and share a resonance with your powerful compassion.

The heart chakra also has strong associations with the natural world and animal queen and kingdoms. Plant, environmental, and animal empaths often have a strong heart chakra, as do those exhibiting strong personality types of the animal whisperer, charity worker, volunteer, support or social worker, carer, companion, healer, therapist, or counselor. The outflow of care, compassion, and unconditional love from the heart chakra reflects in all areas of life and spills out into the other chakras.

The color associated is green.

Throat Chakra

The throat chakra is your communication center. The associated color is blue, and the corresponding element is air. If this chakra becomes blocked, you will experience many problems in your ability to communicate. As an empath who needs expression and freedom to be expressive, this can be very detrimental.

Connected is your heart chakra below and third eye chakra above. Any issues with your sexuality and ability to communicate in intimate relationships will have a strong effect on your heart center, true empathic nature and sense of compassion, and your third-eye center; your ability to perceive subtle energy, connect to a higher power, and use your intuition. The expression of emotion and feelings are paramount to an empath, therefore, keeping a healthy and open throat chakra can be very beneficial in all areas of life. A healthy throat chakra is also essential for those who choose a creative, artistic, or musical path, or for those who go into acting, performing, storytelling of any sort, directing, or speaking. Many empaths find that disruptions and preventions in life before finding their true path are due to an unseen block of energy in one or more of their chakras.

Third Eye or Brow Chakra

This is the seat of consciousness, your higher wisdom and sight center. It is where psychic and intuitive abilities arise and how you can connect to dream states.

By developing this chakra, you can choose partners who can meet you on your frequency. Kindness, caring, compassion, being wise, intuitive and loving: these are all qualities which match your empathic nature. If there is an energy blockage in your third-eye chakra, then your inner knowing will be closed off and you will most likely make choices that are not in harmony with your best interest. It is also the seat of wisdom, knowledge, and power and links to your spiritual sight and awareness. Many spiritual healers, therapists, energy workers, or metaphysically minded empaths, have a strong third eye, as do those who work with dreams and practice paths of shamanism.

The corresponding colors are purple, indigo and violet, and the related element is ether or spirit.

Crown Chakra

Your crown chakra is the seventh major chakra and is located at the top of your head. It is your spiritual connection and responsible for all mystical, transcendental and spiritual experiences. The associated colors are white and gold, and this chakra can be tuned into to enhance all aspects related to psychic and spiritual development.

Regarding sexuality and creativity, if an empath has a healthy and open crown chakra, energy can flow freely down the spine to the root, creating a 'complete circuit.' Disruptions in this chakra can, therefore, have a great effect on all the other chakras.

As the kundalini or serpent, and sexual energy flows from root to crown, this chakra ultimately is responsible for the types of sexual experiences you attract in your life. If the crown is closed, then you are not able to see from a higher awareness, your intuition and perception may be clouded and your emotions 'muddled.' In this respect taking measures to work on the free flow of energy through your crown chakra can heal your sexuality on all levels (so long as the work is done on the other chakras too), which can be a prominent issue for an empath. It also can lead to new levels of imaginative and artistic insight and ideas.

An open and healthy crown chakra is essentially what leads to you living your ultimate and best life, free from psychological and spiritual dysfunction.

The colors and elements relating to the chakras can be connected to and used to enhance any energetic quality you are lacking. As explored in *The Shadow* and *The Wound of the Soul*, there are certain aspects to being an empath which naturally comes with the package. Looking to the chakras, therefore, may be the final step you are seeking in achieving wholeness and harmony within.

It is only once you have created wholeness and harmony within that you can truly be a gift for others, and shine and reflect your inner light out to the world.

How to Heal Your Chakras: A Short Exercise

Now you are familiar with your chakras and what they correspond to, you can incorporate this exercise into daily life to help you on your journey to wholeness. This exercise can be used for all of your chakras and is particularly effective at working through any problems associated with being an empath on a deeper level. This may include over-emotionalism, over-sensitivity, unprotected boundaries, or picking up and absorbing things which are not yours.

- Create a sacred space. Create a sacred space and get in a meditative position. Candles, incense or a resin-like frankincense, essential oils, and some symbolic items such as a flower or special gemstone (earth), a shell or bowl of water (water), a candle (fire) and a feather (air) can be used to enhance the effectiveness of this exercise.

- Close your eyes and focus on your breath. Create an inner space and bring your awareness inside. Sync your breath to a calm and steady rate and become peaceful within, aware of your surroundings.

- Bring your hands up to your heart and rub them together slightly, energizing your palms. Now bring them together facing each other in front of your heart but not touching. Now imagine a ball of glowing light growing between your palms (the color is the associated chakra you are working on). Keep your focus on your breath while simultaneously watching this ball of loving light grow and expand.

- Set your intention on cultivating, developing, and increasing the qualities you wish to heal and integrate. For example, if your glowing light is green, you can focus your intent on empathy, kindness, and self-love. If it is blue, the characteristics could be calmness of being, perfect communication, and peaceful expression.

- Visualize your chosen qualities grow inside the expanding ball of energy. Really feel them there and allow yourself to feel their presence.

- Finally, once you feel a connection with both the qualities and the color, slowly bring your ball of light up to the associated chakra and pour it over you. Visualize it going into you and filling your energy body and physical body with these beautiful qualities. Don't rush it. Make a connection and breathe deeply into this feeling.

- End the exercise by rubbing your hands together to close the circuit and resting your hands on your knees in a meditative position. Slowly come into your body allowing yourself to feel all the various sensations and emotions.

Kundalini and Wholeness: The Journey of Completion

As you are aware by now your mind, body, and spirit are designed to work in harmony. Your thoughts affect your emotions and spiritual health just as your emotional well being affects your spiritual awareness and mental health. For an empath like yourself, life is a holistic experience. This means that when part of yourself is not functioning, neither is another part. Being an empath can be a rich and emotionally rewarding experience, yet it can also leave you feeling drained and cut off from the world, despite your deep emotional connection.

This brings us to kundalini and wholeness within. As shared in the previous section, your chakras are very real and deeply powerful portals of energy. They relate to your physical systems just as they equally link to some psychological, emotional and spiritual aspect of self. Your kundalini, therefore, is the *unified, whole and balanced state*, the free flow of energy from root to crown. Your kundalini is in a state of flow when your chakras are in harmony, balanced and energized. As an empath, this is the source of your spiritual gifts.

Intuition, advanced creative and artistic ability, imagination, empathic genius, perceptions and insight, spiritual awareness, and a sense of enlightenment all come with having a healed and activated kundalini. Your unique compassion, natural kindness, and unconditional love, and under and innerstanding of others come with this. It can, therefore, be seen that the ultimate goal of the empath is to reach your highest vibratory state psychologically and spiritually, so you can live your best life and fulfill your own sense of soul purpose, whatever that may be.

Using the techniques, tips and guidance throughout these chapters can help you do this.

In the words of Maya Angelou: "I think we all have empathy. We may not have the *courage* to display it."

Conclusion

'Intuitive Empath' takes you on a journey of *inner*standing helping you to define and integrate what it means to be an empath. Combining both spiritual awareness and scientific backing, a heart-centered approach is offered, with the intention to act as your guide to psychological and spiritual healing and wholeness.

Empathy is a beautiful gift. These chapters aim to help you make sense of it.

References

The Science Behind Empathy and Empaths. (2019). Retrieved from https://www.psychologytoday.com/gb/blog/the-empaths-survival-guide/201703/the-science-behind-empathy-and-empaths

(2019). Retrieved from https://journals.lww.com/psychosoma

PsycNET. (2019). Retrieved from https://psycnet.apa.org/record/2008-14857-004

PsycNET. (2019). Retrieved from https://psycnet.apa.org/record/2008-13989-015

Staff, C. (2019). Enhancing Compassion: A Randomized Controlled Trial of a Compassion Cultivation Training Program - The Center for Compassion and Altruism Research and Education. Retrieved from http://ccare.stanford.edu/article/enhancing-compassion-a-randomized-controlled-trial-of-a-compassion-cultivation-training/